CW01188134

PIAGET

© 2010 Assouline Publishing
601 West 26th Street, 18th floor
New York, NY 10001, USA
Tel.: 212 989-6810   Fax: 212 647-0005
www.assouline.com

This book combines and updates the previous Assouline editions
Piaget (2000) and *Piaget Jewellery* (2001).
Translated from the French by Linda Jarosiewicz.
ISBN: 978 2 7594 0461 2

Color separation by Planète Couleurs (France)
Printed by Grafiche Milani (Italy)

All rights reserved.
No part of this publication may be reproduced, stored in a retrieval system,
or transmitted in any form or by any means, electronic, mechanical,
photocopying, recording, or otherwise, without prior consent from the publisher.

PIAGET

FRANCO COLOGNI

Today, authentic luxury lies in giving meaning to time.

Sheep and fairies

The heraldic crest of the village of La Côte-aux-Fées has a sheep on it, from which it can be deduced that the hill on which Piaget's native village stands does not belong to the fairies (*fées*) but rather to the sheep, or *fayes,* as these placid animals are called in the local dialect. Be that as it may, both sheep and fairies are village emblems: the sheep are a reminder of the hard work of the shepherds and the peasant farmers; the fairies evoke the naive popular imagination, the dreams, and the pleasures that refresh body and soul after long hours of weary toil.

Sheep and fairies, labour and pleasure also symbolize Piaget: proud of its roots, faithful to its origins, a house that, like few others, has been able to reconcile dreams and reality, expertise and aesthetics.

Lace and watches

The winters are harsh in La Côte-aux-Fées, as they are in all the valleys of the Swiss Canton Jura that are so lush and green in spring. The snow-covered fields cannot be worked for several months of each year.

In this region, marked by the sermons of the Reformation, sloth is the least tolerated of the deadly sins. Canton Neuchâtel, to which La Côte-aux-Fées belongs, was part of a region won over by the teachings of Guillaume Farel (1489–1565). This French Lutheran iconoclast and disciple of Ulrich Zwingli settled in Geneva, to which he later summoned John Calvin.

When the Swiss Jura joined the Reformation, customs became even more austere, and idleness even rarer. The long winter months were spent developing crafts such as lacemaking and later watchmaking —activities that alternated with agriculture and stockbreeding in step with the seasons. In the mid-nineteenth century, watchmaking supplanted lacemaking once and for all.

Split parts

From then onward, the Swiss Jura became a vast haven of specialized craftsmen who continuously supplied the *manufactures d'horlogerie* (watchmaking manufacturers) in Geneva, the undisputed capital of the industry. This organizational model, deeply rooted in the region, was based on watch production divided into "split parts," thus enabling each home-based craftsman to become extremely specialized.

In the 1870s, when a serious crisis created by competition from the United States forced Swiss watchmakers to undertake a radical reorganization of their profession, the verticalization of production to create in-house *manufactures* aroused little interest among the most prestigious brands. The latter continued to make the most of the existing network of small, highly specialized workshops, which ensured incomparable quality.

The indispensability of the most qualified craftsmen was firmly established. Thanks to their flexibility and expertise, their small cottage industries became the hub of technical and aesthetic innovation, while more run-of-the-mill output became concentrated in large production facilities.

Such was the highly specialized socioeconomic context in which Georges Edouard Piaget, at the tender age of nineteen, founded the company that still bears his name to this day.

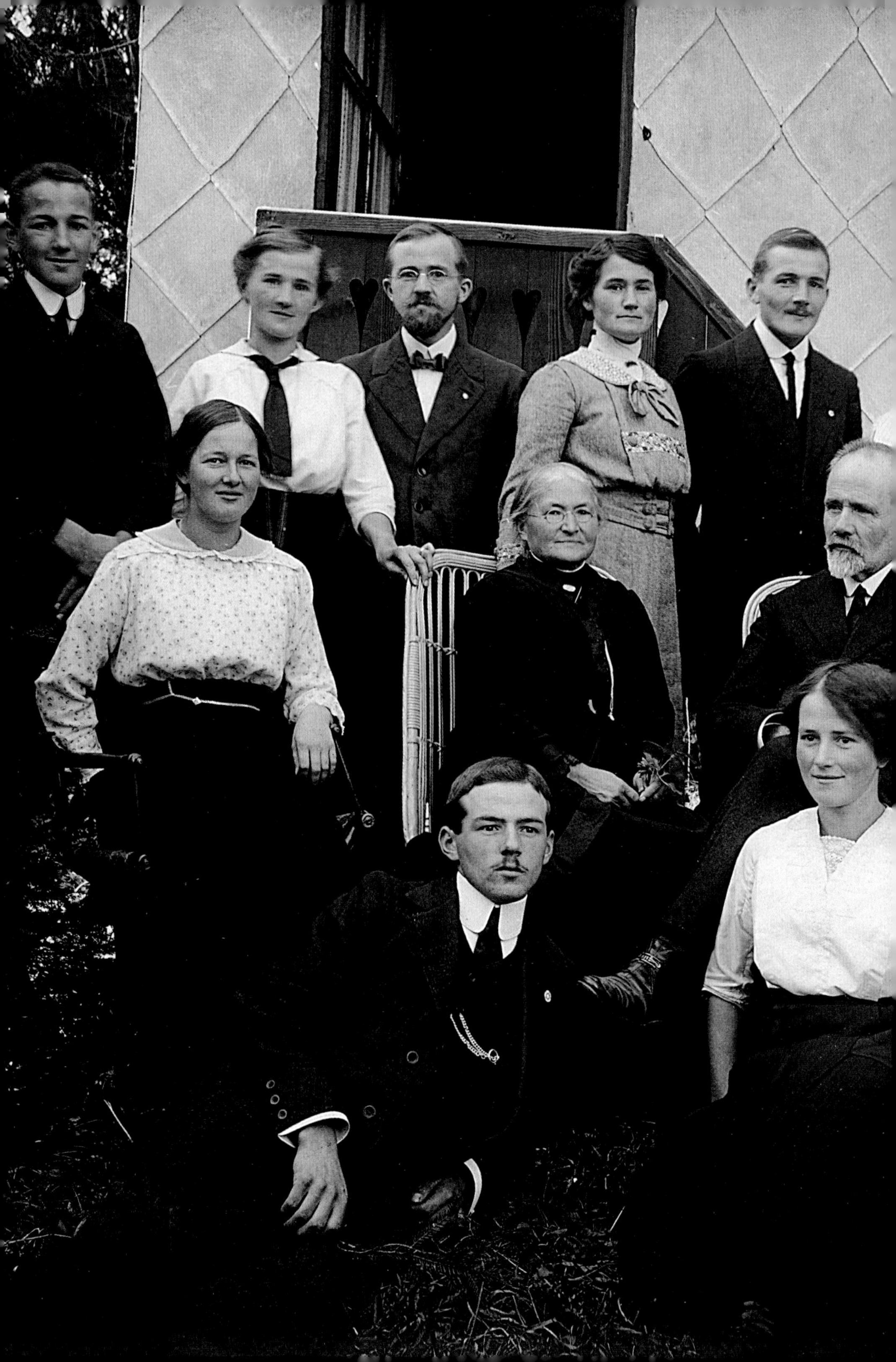

Roots

Trade secrets

In La Côte-aux-Fées, and throughout Canton Neuchâtel, Piaget is a common name, as indeed is the watchmaking trade.
There were Piaget watchmakers well before 1874: the firm's private collection has four watches signed "Piaget", made between 1820 and 1836 and therefore before the House of Piaget was founded. Perhaps they were crafted by a relative of the young Georges Edouard Piaget, who was himself an apprentice in the small workshop of a watchmaker in Les Bayards, a village near his home.
He quickly learned all the secrets of the trade and, from among the possible specializations, he opted for the lever escapement which, in addition to its undeniable technical qualities, made it possible for him to develop extremely thin movements.

Expertise and humility

Georges Edouard Piaget achieved excellent results. By 1911, when his workshop had to be abandoned for larger premises in order to accommodate his many employees, his name was well known by all the top Swiss brands. Over time, the Piagets came to specialize in the production of complete mechanisms and even finished watches, which clients engraved with their own brand names. This extremely skilled work was done humbly and anonymously. Throughout the decades of the early twentieth century, the House of Piaget did not sign its watches or its movements.
By 1885, Georges, who had married Emma Bünzli in 1881, already had four heirs, including three sons—a promising start, as the

couple would go on to have fourteen children. The custom of the time was for the living quarters (on the ground floor) and the workshops (on the better-lit upper floors) to be housed under the same roof, with everyone living and working together. In the Swiss Jura, another principle was also considered extremely important: talent was always more valuable than any rights acquired by birth.

Therefore, also in 1911, when Georges decided to retire at the age of fifty-six, he handed the reins over to young Timothée. He was only the fourth child, and the third son, but he was the best watchmaker in the brood. At this time, the small family firm became a general partnership company made up of Georges Edouard himself, his brother William, and, in addition to Timothée, the two elder sons, Edouard and Georges.

Moving to the city

In the years between the two world wars, the small workshop created by Georges Edouard Piaget (who died in 1931 at the age of 76) became a full-fledged business.

Geneva was now an international city. It had welcomed the French Huguenots in the sixteenth century; the Great Exhibition in 1896 brought it into the modern age; but it truly emerged onto the international stage after the First World War, with the creation of the League of Nations. Starting in 1920, a vibrant, elegant social life was organized around this league and the political elite drawn to Geneva by the new institution.

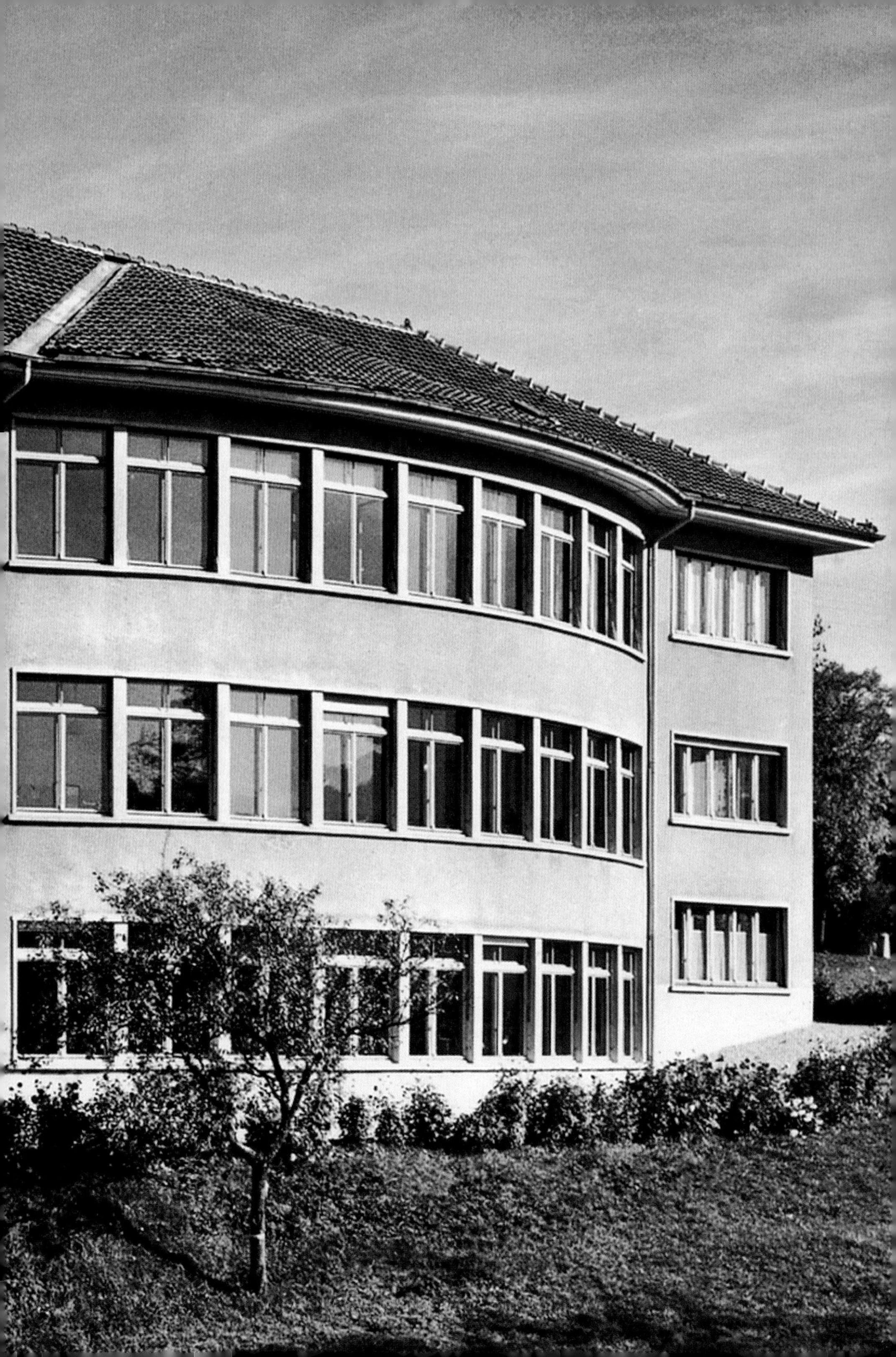

PIAGET
SWITZERLAND

Watches and jewellery in which Geneva had always specialized, attracted a top-notch international clientele. The broad, airy quaysides along the lake were resplendent with boutique windows filled with gleaming gold and precious gems. At the time, Geneva was home to Piaget's most important clients, famous watchmakers and jewellers to royal courts the world over, so they naturally often travelled to the city.

Perhaps it was Timothée who was the first to dream before the display windows where watches were transformed into sparkling wonders of light, the first to conceive of the bold project that in only a few years would transform the La Côte-aux-Fées workshop into one of the world's most famous watch and jewellery companies.

Taking off

In 1945, Timothée Piaget also retired and a third-generation Piaget became the head of the company. Timothée had twelve heirs, two of whom would prove to be authentic geniuses, each in his own field, and would jointly lead the house along the road to success.

Gérald was responsible for sales. A great traveller, he was able to establish a vast network of connections with clients and future distributors. Valentin was the designer and the master watchmaker, following in the footsteps of his grandfather but with his own genius —an innate talent that can never be acquired or passed on.

In 1940, impelled by the more open ideas and bolder projects of the new generation, Piaget started to sign its watches. After sixty-six years of existence, this was no random decision.

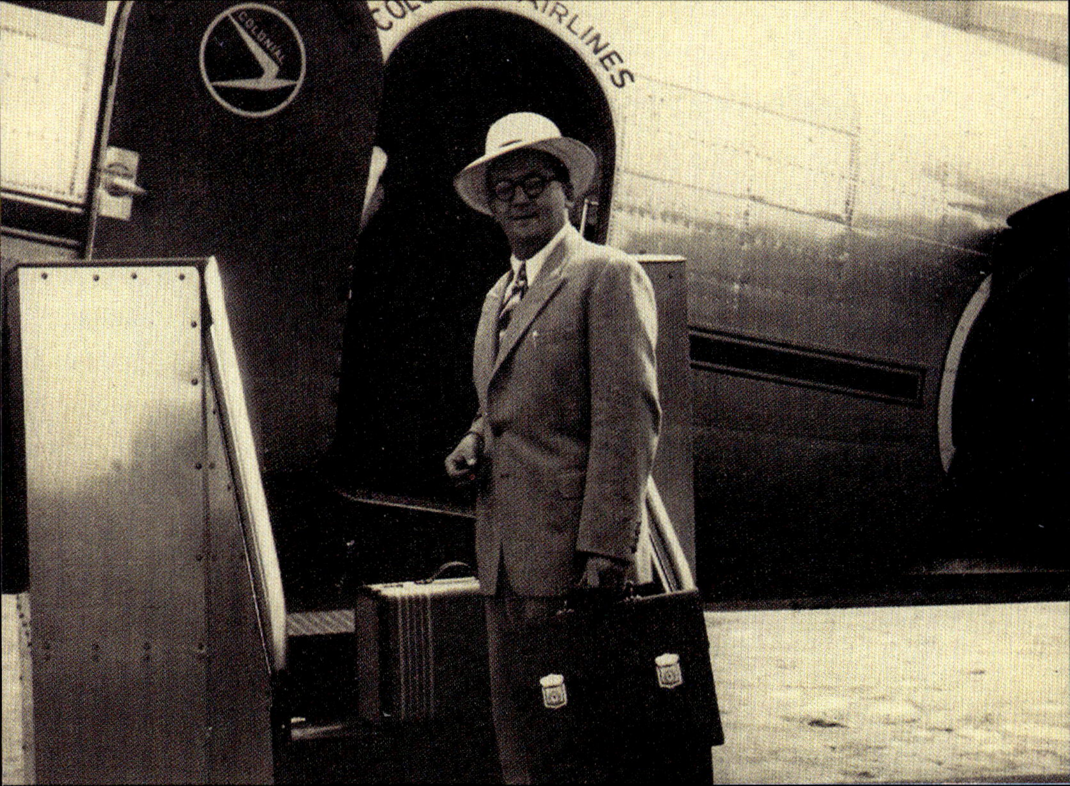
AIRLINES

The year that Timothée passed the reins to Gérald (assisted by Valentin as deputy director and Camille Pilet as international sales manager) also marked the inauguration of the company's new workshop facility. Established in La Côte-aux-Fées, it was designed for manufacturing state-of-the-art timepieces. The ultramodern complex was intended to house more than two hundred specialized craftsmen, far more than the village could offer at the time. The history of the house was gathering pace.

The ultra-thin revolution

"Luxury and Precision" was the slogan chosen by Piaget for its creations in 1942. Having joined the business, Gérald and Valentin wanted their brand to reach the pinnacle of watchmaking, both in quality and price. This choice, deemed to be suicidal by their competitors until the end of the 1950s, turned out, on the contrary, to have been both courageous and visionary.

During these same years, two events of major importance marked a decisive turning point in the history of the house and contributed to justifying this decision: the development in 1956 of Calibre 9P, a mechanical movement that was only two millimeters thick, and its introduction at the 1957 Basel Watch Fair.

Designed and created thanks to Valentin's clear-sighted intelligence, this movement revolutionized the watchmaking market, in particular, ladies' watches. Although women wanted thinner watches suited to their wrists, the models they were being offered were monstrously bulky. Calibre 9P made it possible to greatly increase the size of watch faces while still offering a very elegant profile. Piaget had once and for all acquired the status of a fine watchmaking house.

PIAGET Spécialistes des montres les plus plates du mond[e]

Dans l'esprit de l'homme
et de la femme distingués
aucun compromis n'est possible.
Elégance et précision forment
une entité : l'essence même
de la distinction.
Cette particularité s'applique
aux montres Piaget, créations
exclusives dues au génie artistique
de l'horloger-artisan suisse.

Piaget, la montre de
l'élite du monde.
Vente exclusive auprès
des meilleurs joailliers.

PIAGET
Symbole de perfection depuis 1874

The Piaget boutique

Without abandoning the village that had ensured the excellence of the *manufacture*, with its tradition of high-quality craftsmanship, the Piaget brothers opened a boutique at 40, rue du Rhône in Geneva—one of the most prestigious locations in the city—where the brand is still represented today. The showroom was inaugurated on June 15, 1959.

On that day, a handsome young seventeen-year-old stopped in front of the elegant window. He found it impossible to tear himself away from the sight and even glued his nose to the glass to get a better view of what was inside. In truth, there was little to see, apart from a few exceptional watches driven by mechanisms that held no secrets for the adolescent. His attention was fixed on the boutique itself rather than on the precious objects on display there, intended to catch the gaze of passersby.

A window opening onto a fascinating world, the place impressed the young man, who was none other than Yves G. Piaget, the scion of the fourth generation of the family of Neuchâtel watchmakers and the heir to an exceptional legacy of expertise and invention. His dream was not simply to purchase one of the wonders on display for himself but rather to one day give an international dimension to the brand that carried his name. He saw himself at the the helm of the company, transforming it into a temple of luxury, ready to compete with the greatest watchmakers in Geneva.

But for the time being, young Yves still lived in La Côte-aux-Fées, the Jura village where he was born, a village where success did not go to one's head. His entire family was from the village. The Piagets were strict moralists and somewhat parsimonious, like most mountain dwellers, especially those in a Protestant region. Therefore, a seventeen-year-old boy was expected to stick to his appointed place. He was not yet mature, and his duty was to learn to acquire maturity. Yves would learn quickly.

A decade of triumph

The showroom in Geneva was first and foremost intended to stand up to the competition. It was unimaginable that so luxurious a store as the one on the rue du Rhône, with such clearly affirmed ambitions, would be content to sell nothing but watches—especially after clients began regularly requesting jewellery and accessories to match the watches they had just purchased.

The Piagets therefore decided to source jewellery from the finest Parisian jewellers, as well as from Italy and Germany, and to put their name on it. These objects created by others would allow the family to enrich and diversify its range of products in order to satisfy a clientele that was becoming increasingly demanding.

The 1960s was a triumphant decade for Piaget. Valentin decided to create small display cases in which a minimum number of pieces were shown, while competitors presented a large number of watches in vast display cases. The interior of the Piaget boutique was furnished like a living room, with no products in view. From outside, passersby could see no watches or jewellery, only armchairs, sofas, and elegant side tables. Visitors were served some of the best coffee in Geneva, accompanied by the finest chocolates — products made exclusively for Piaget that were savoured in plush havens of luxury.

Corporate policy regarding jewellery took a whole new turn. The era of purchasing ready-made pieces from jewellers and simply placing the brand's logo on them was now over. Henceforth, Piaget jewellery was to be exclusive, personalized, and specially designed. It would soon be created by the same craftspeople who already cut the semiprecious stones for the watch faces and set the diamonds in the watch cases and bracelets.

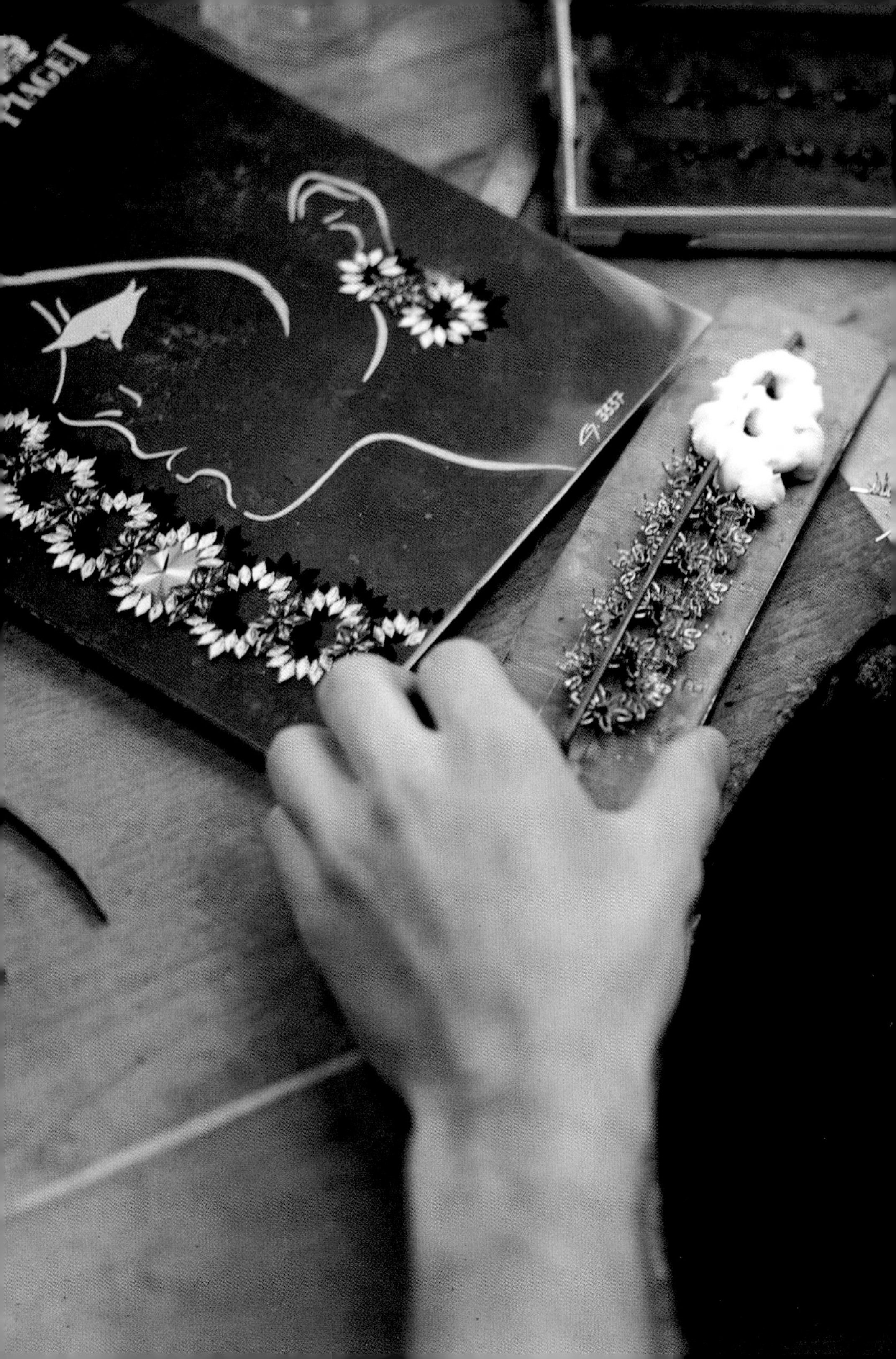
PIAGET

PIAGET

Noble metals and an aristocratic clientele

Alongside the existing "Luxury and Precision" motto, another slogan appeared in a 1957 brand catalogue: "Piaget, the Watch of the International Elite." This underscored the clear-sighted talent for marketing displayed by Piaget in pursuing its goal of becoming the watchmaker and jeweller of the international elite. That same year, Piaget proudly proclaimed its decision to produce watches made from noble metals (gold and platinum) to the exclusion of any other metals, thus affirming its vocation as a jeweller. Considering that in 1966, less than ten years after this announcement, the company had reached a production level of ten thousand such precious items, it is easy to understand that this challenge, initially greeted with skepticism, ended up astounding the competition. After all, the use of steel was widespread, even among top-of-the-line brands. Piaget was now part of the limited circle of distinguished houses that give luxury its true meaning.

The subtle charm of a movement

Just three years after the introduction of Calibre 9P, Valentin Piaget developed another revolutionary movement. Presented at the 1960 Basel Watch Fair, Calibre 12P, the thinnest self-winding movement in the world at the time, drew a host of curious observers. Among them were a large number of experts from Piaget's rival companies, which was the most flattering praise the brand could receive. While some observers doubted that a movement just 2.3 millimetres thick could really be automatic, the influential *Journal de Genève* newspaper was dazzled and stated that the creation of Calibre 12P constituted a watershed event in watchmaking history.

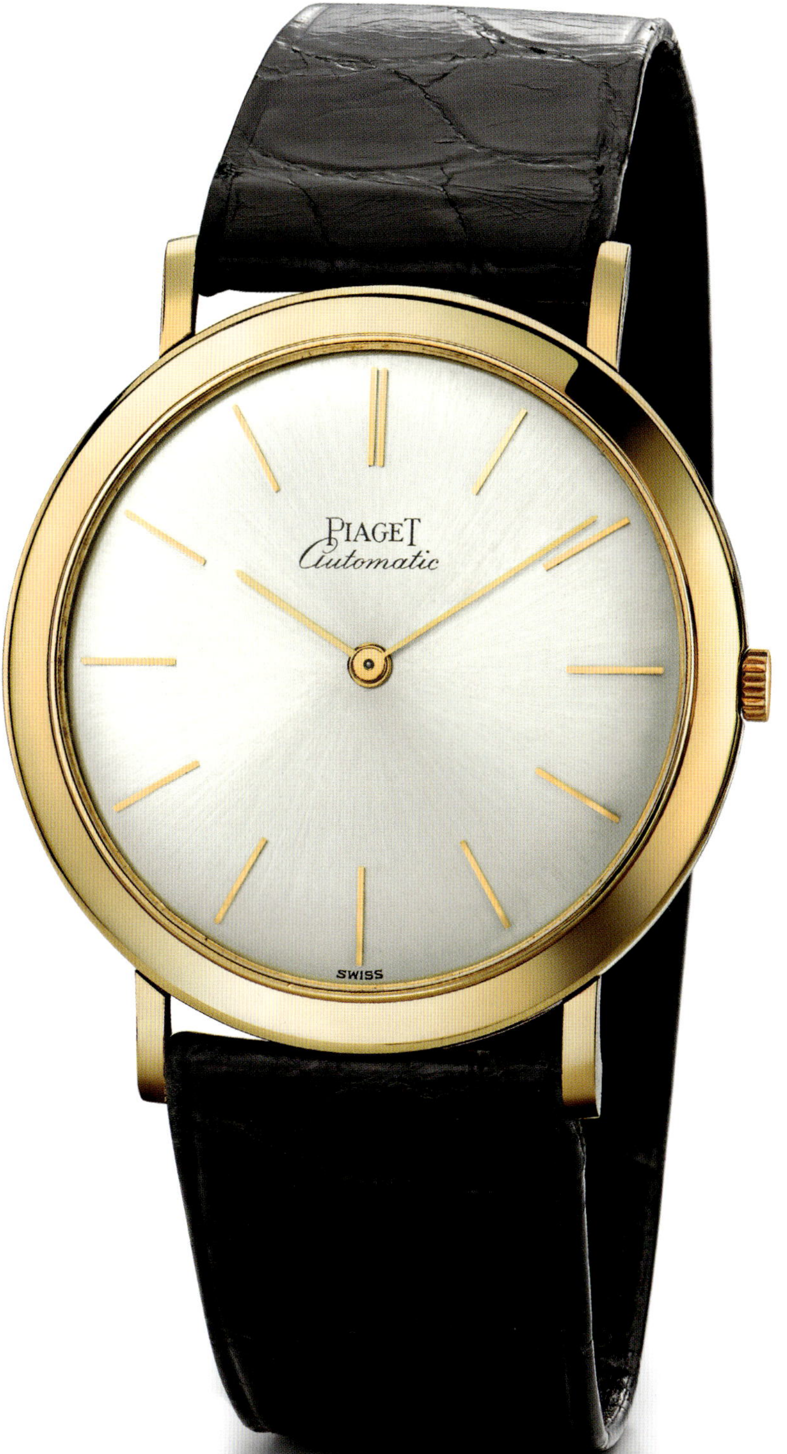
PIAGET
Automatic
SWISS

PIAGET

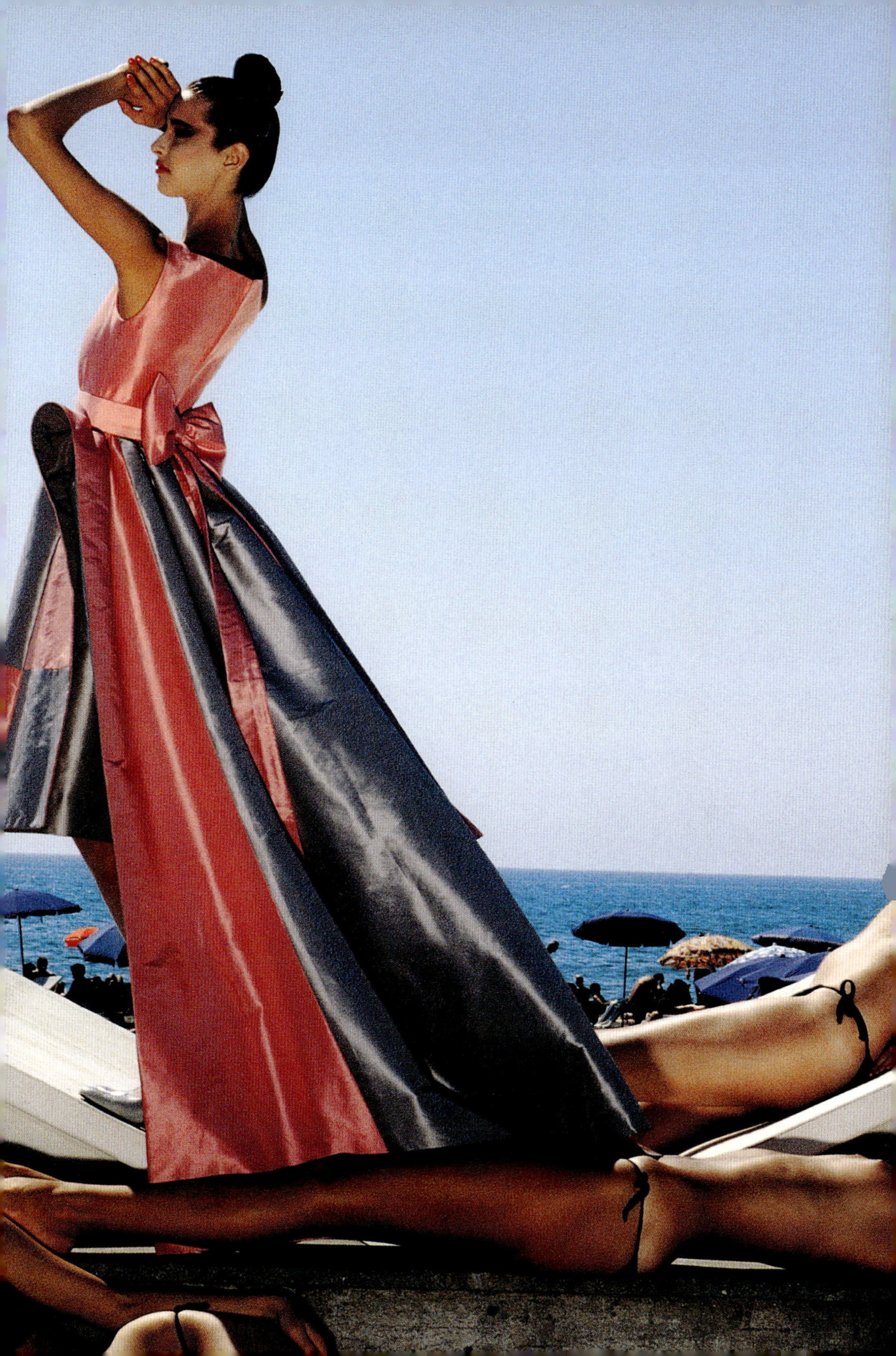

Fanciful wrist-worn extravagance

The 1960s was the wildest, most creative, most original, and most nonconformist decade of the twentieth century. In the watchmaking industry, Piaget was brilliantly able to interpret the whimsical, rebellious spirit of the times.

Although the two ultra-thin calibres were technical feats in themselves, the real revolution was in the aesthetic freedom that they offered. The imagination of company designers was unleashed and expressed itself through bezels and bracelets sparkling with diamonds, sapphires, rubies, and emeralds. Watches became jewellery creations.

The brand's reputation and its vocation as a watchmaker-jeweller were now assured. The most prestigious jewellers around the world —from Asprey & Garrard in London to Tiffany & Co. in New York, and from Cartier in Paris to Bulgari in Rome—welcomed Piaget watches into their collections. In a short time, due to their intrinsic value and incomparable, innovative aesthetics, the inimitable "Piaget look" became the watch of the jet set, the upper class, and the stars. Just glance through the newsweeklies and the women's magazines published at the start of the 1960s: personalities such as Jackie

Kennedy Onassis; movie stars such as Sophia Loren and Gina Lollobrigida, and singers such as Maurice Chevalier and Mireille Mathieu all wore a Piaget watches on their wrist.

Colour makes a splash

Piaget did not stop there and, in 1964, launched an innovative idea: watches with dials made from hard or semiprecious stones. Colour reigned supreme, with materials such as jade, lapis lazuli, malachite, tigereye, opal, onyx, and turquoise. The variety was almost infinite, with no less than thirty different stones listed in the company's catalogue.
Confirming its vocation as a jeweller, Piaget created unique watches, each instantly becoming a collector's item.
Due to the inevitability of slightly different tints, unequal striations, and inclusions, the use of hard stones meant that no two watches could ever be identical.

Wise savings and sound investments

Although they remained loyal to a strict Calvinist moral code and practiced the careful stewardship inculcated by their rural upbringing by being parsimonious within their own family, Gérald and Valentin spared no expense as far as the company was concerned. When it was more advantageous and provident to loosen their purse strings rather than to tighten them, they did so.
Therefore, in 1964, assisted by Camille Pilet and Emil Keller (another personality identified with the house), they acquired Baume & Mercier.

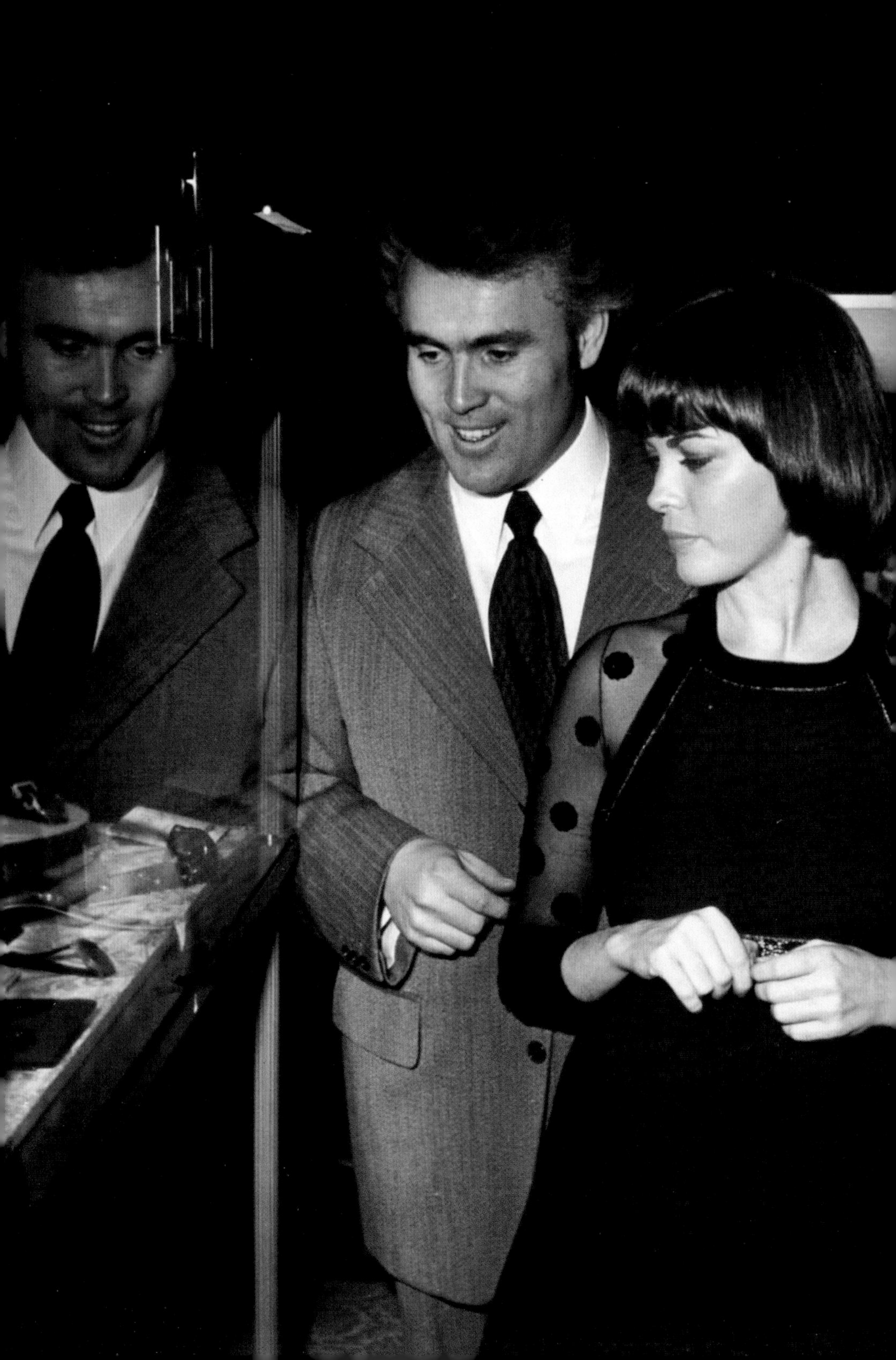

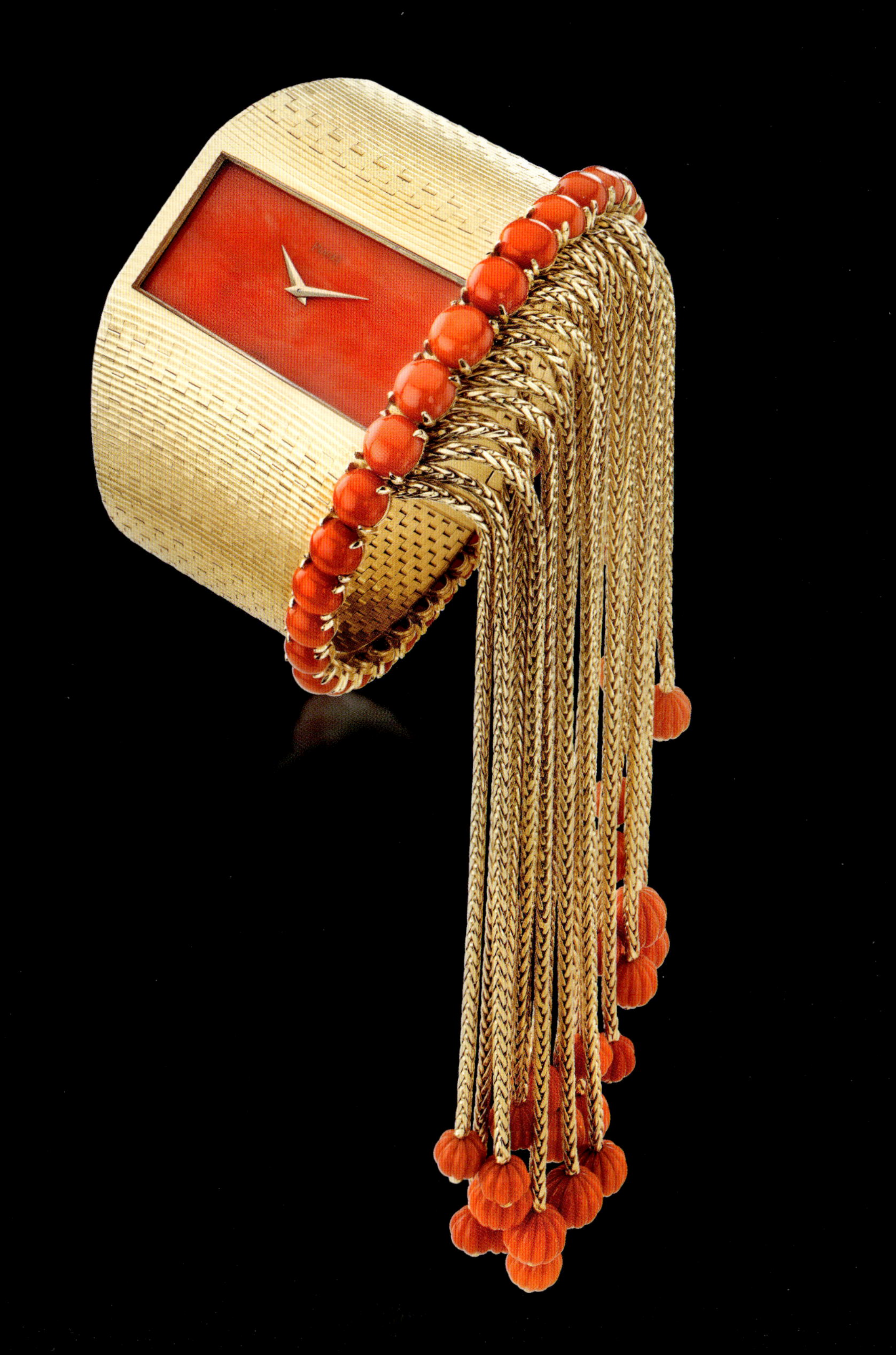

Founded in 1830, this brand gained international fame at the end of the nineteenth century for its precision chronometers and established itself in the 1920s and '30s with the production of a broad range of models, great competitiveness, and a corporate spirit based on the values of knowledge and expertise.

Interpreting the Piaget look

Meanwhile, Gérald's son, Yves G. Piaget, had followed his father's advice by studying in accordance with family tradition, earning a degree as a watchmaking engineer from the University of Neuchâtel and another as a graduate gemologist from the Gemological Institute of America in Los Angeles. In 1966, he returned to Europe and began working in the family business at the age of twenty-five. He was appointed marketing and communications director in 1968, but first he had to prove himself as a simple employee at the boutique on the rue du Rhône. His salary was barely enough to pay the rent on a studio apartment and to buy his first car, a Fiat 500 which, like the precious items produced by the house, showed originality in its design.

Having honed his knowledge of the tastes and expectations of international clients during his spell at the Geneva boutique, Yves decided to take a hand in the designing of pieces of jewellery.

He had some formidable assets: the experience acquired through direct contact with the company's clientele and his natural ease with people. Soon he started regularly visiting the most famous and creative jewellers in Europe. He was searching for artists who were able to provide sensitive interpretations of the already famous "Piaget look" watches that were conquering the jet set.

Each time he was won over by an interesting idea that matched his requirements, Yves G. Piaget acquired it, reworked it with the model-maker in order to give it the Piaget touch, and produced an exclusive piece. He also chose workshops according to their various specializations in order to obtain the best quality and the most perfect craftsmanship.

Homage to the diamond

In parallel, Piaget produced *haute joaillerie* creations that were both refined and precious, created as one-of-a-kind models or in limited series. Inspired by the daring creativity of its watches, Piaget jewellery conferred genuine nobility on semiprecious stones by giving them a contemporary interpretation, while never neglecting or failing to honour traditional precious stones, particularly diamonds.

The Piagets reconciled tradition with classicism, with a creative boldness that put them ahead of fashion trends. On one hand, they were not afraid to experiment with materials seldom used in jewellery, and on the other, they followed to the letter the self-imposed rule established in 1957: never to use anything other than gold or platinum, for both watches and jewellery, a strategic choice that sometimes garnered sneers from their competitors.

However, multimillionaires, artists, and jet-setting women were charmed and enthusiastically welcomed the aesthetic revolution boldly introduced by the Genevan house, of which Yves G. Piaget was the dedicated ambassador. It was his custom to personally present the house's creations to the most celebrated personalities of the time, such as Elizabeth Taylor and Richard Burton, who had a chalet in Gstaad.

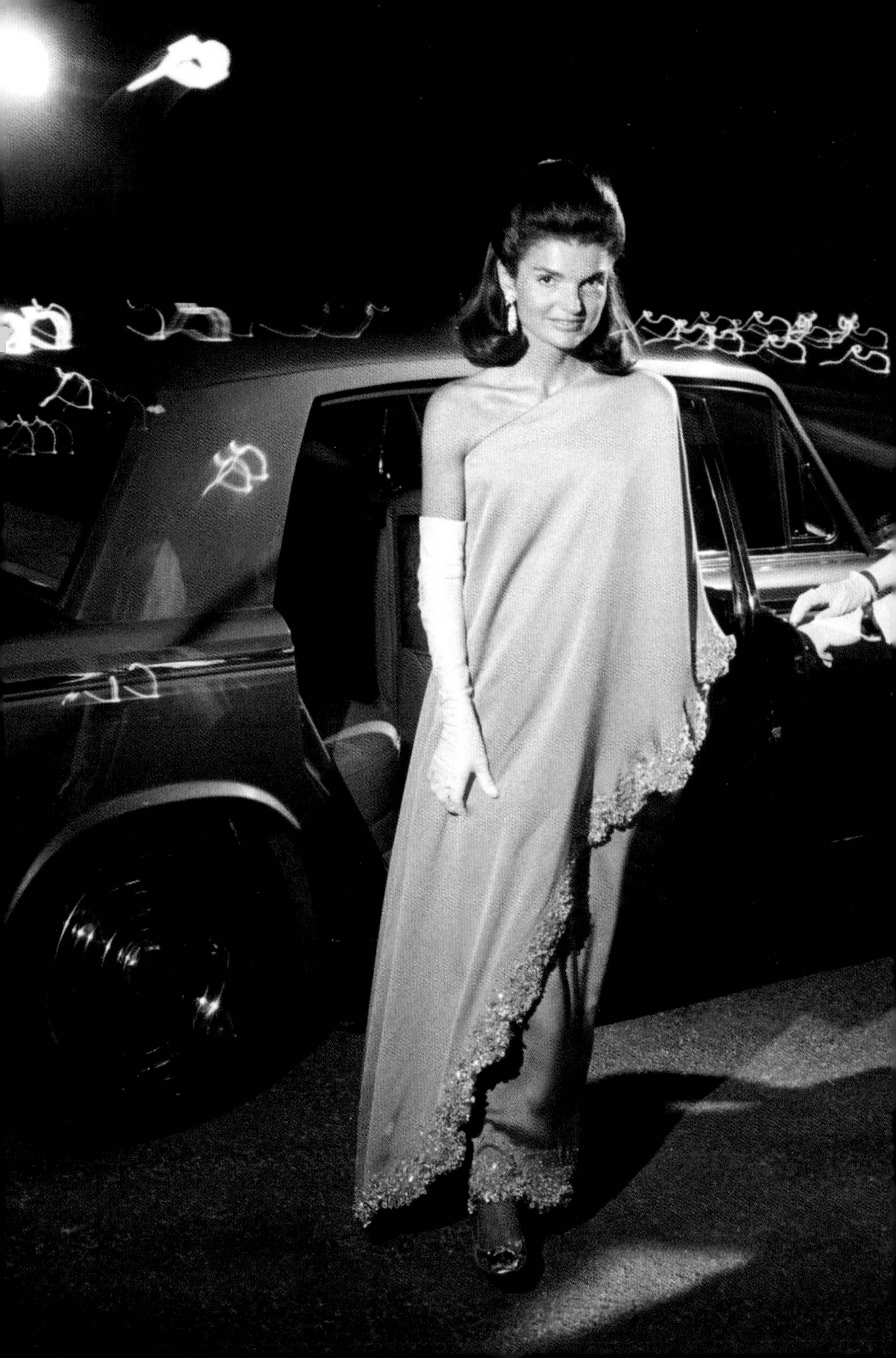

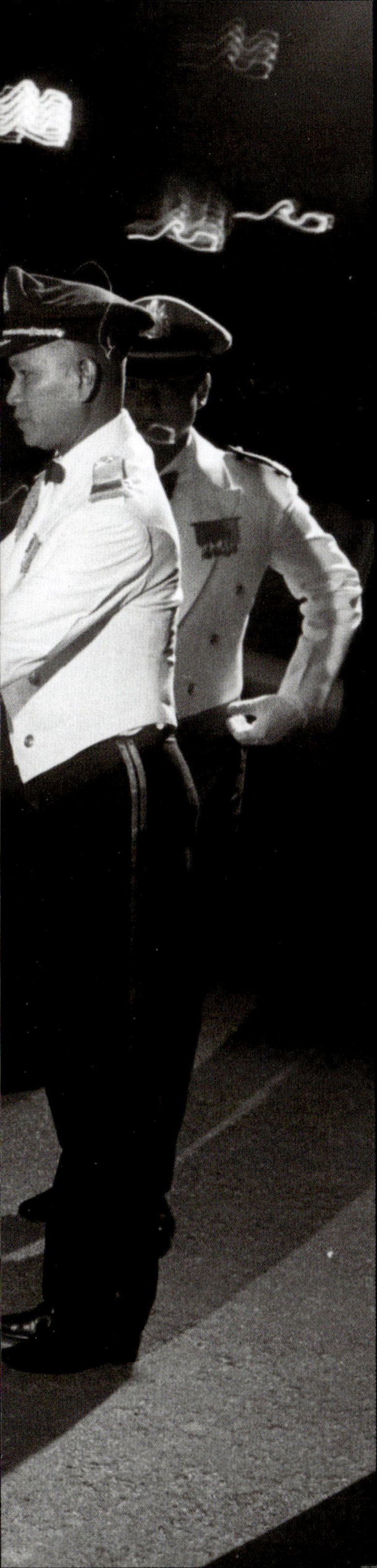

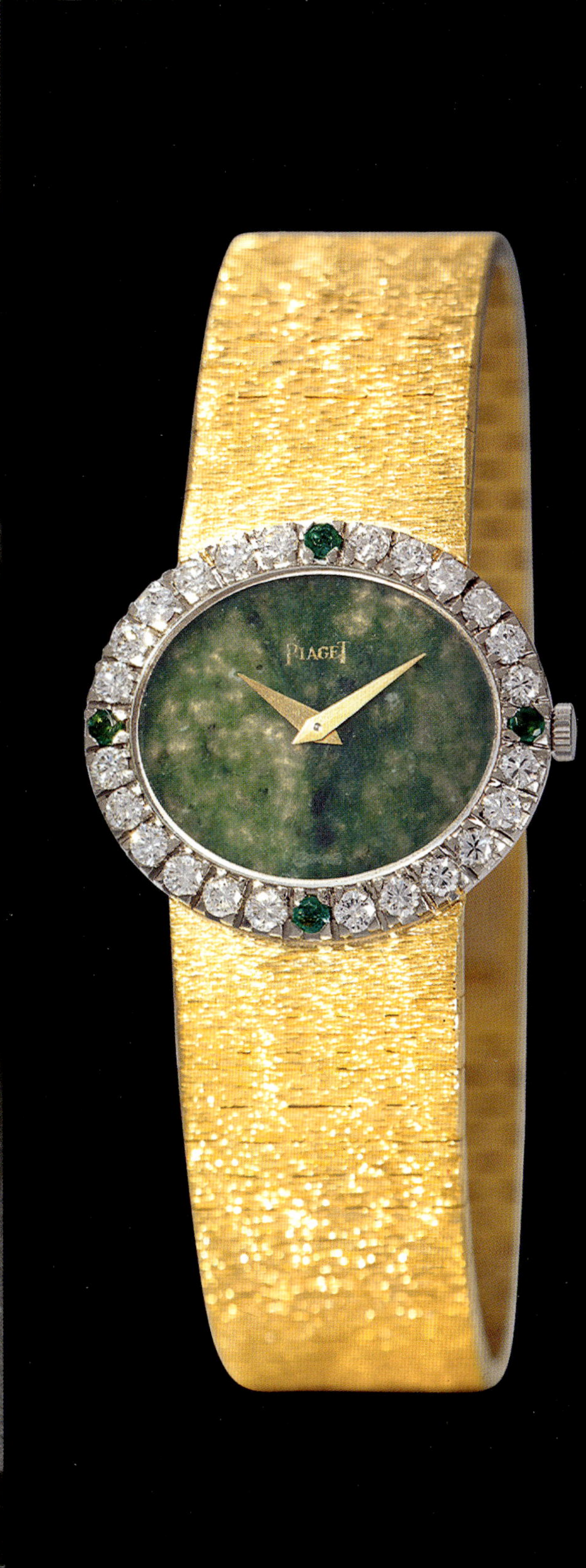
PIAGET

A jeweller in its own right

Piaget was no longer simply the jeweller of watchmaking but was now a jeweller in its own right. In 1961, it began consolidating its status by purchasing specialized workshops so as to better control the production process. This represented a further step along the path to becoming identified as a jeweller.

To celebrate the company's centenary in 1974, Piaget opened the Prodor jewellery-making and goldsmiths' workshops in Geneva, created to integrate the fabrication of watch cases and bracelets, as well as gem-setting operations. Thanks to the outstanding skills of its artisans, truly extraordinary jewellery and watches were to be designed and created there. The Piaget style became a signature code that would attract a worldwide clientele which was keenly aware of "the difference."

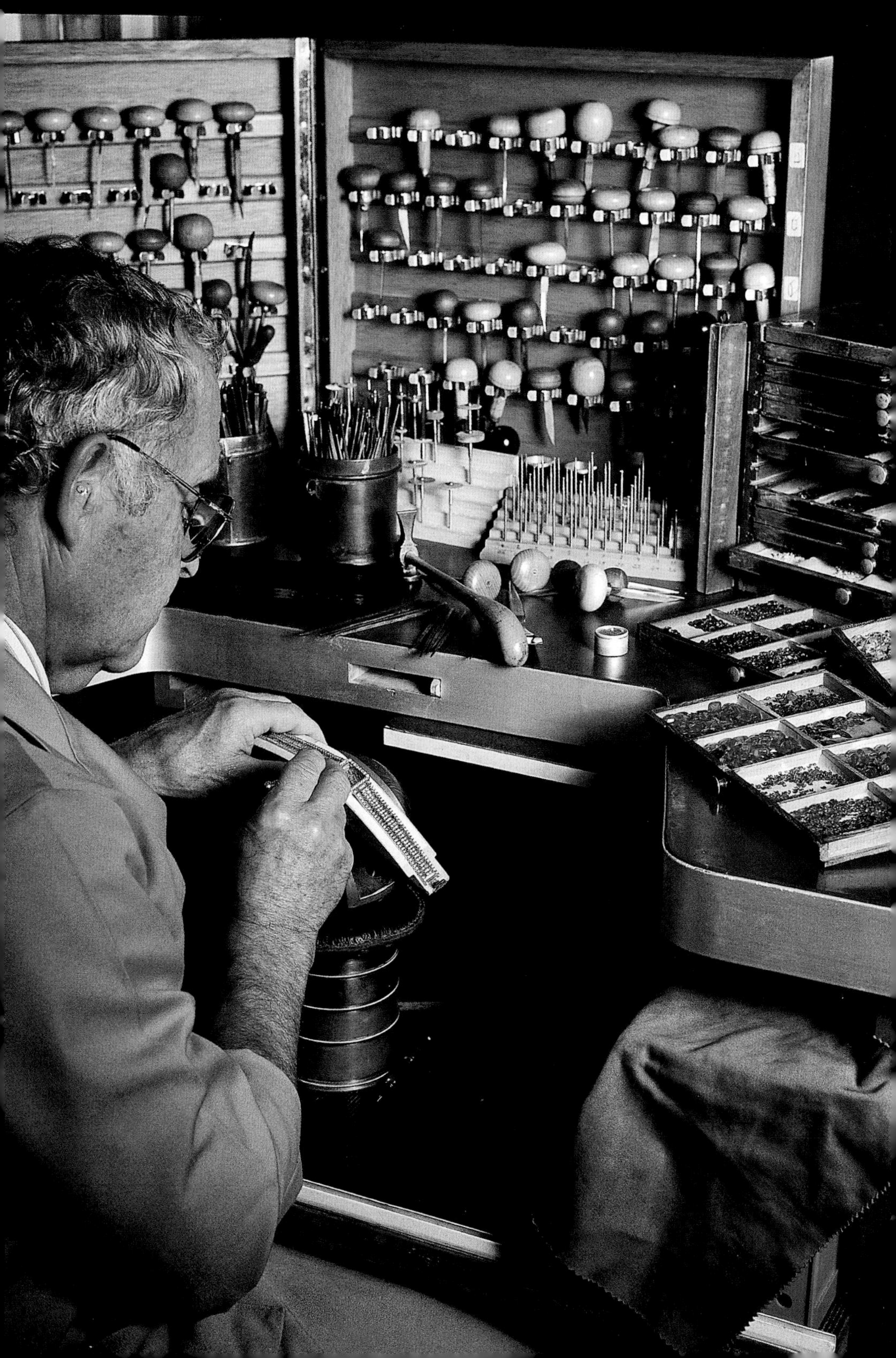

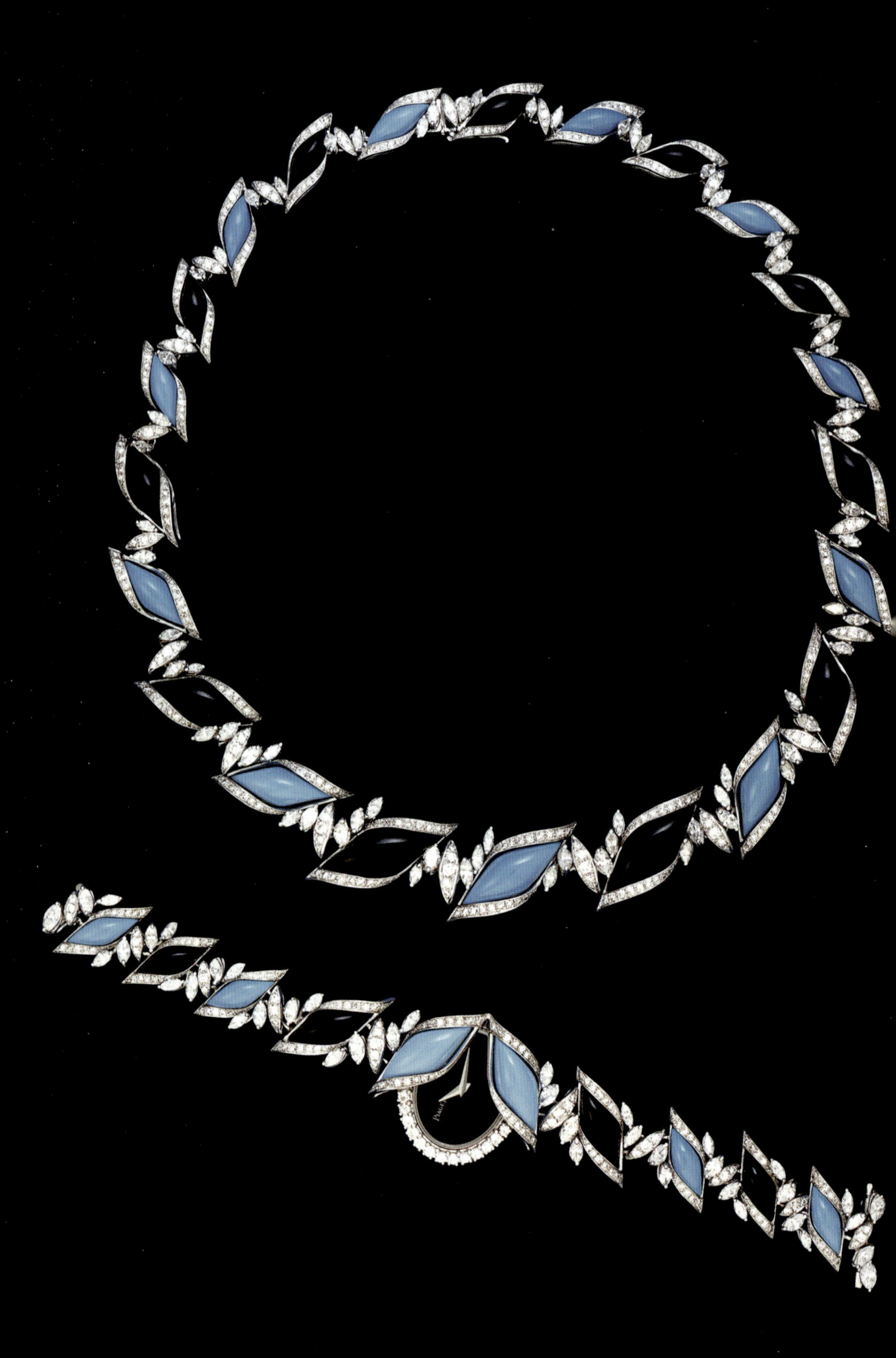

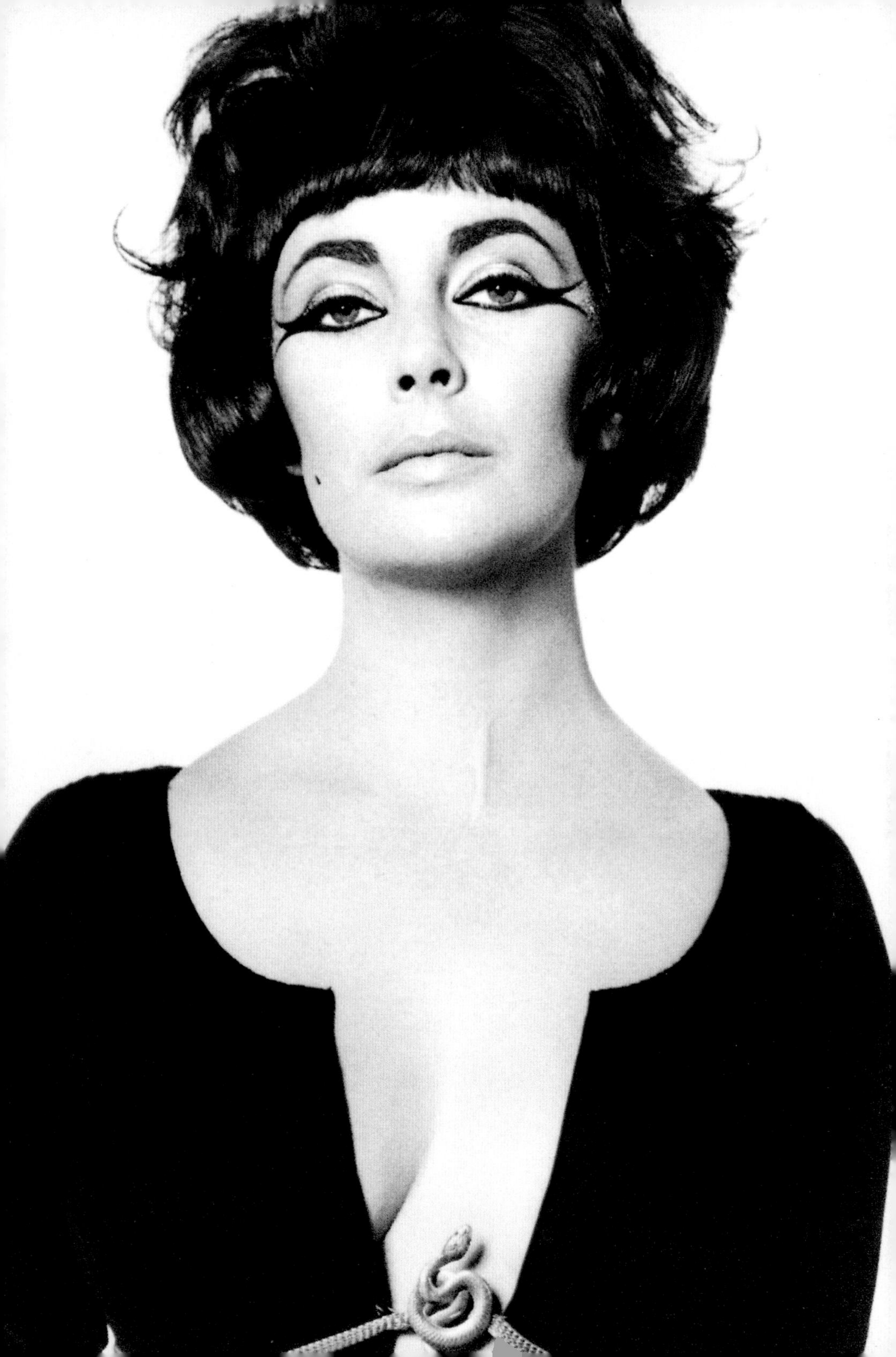

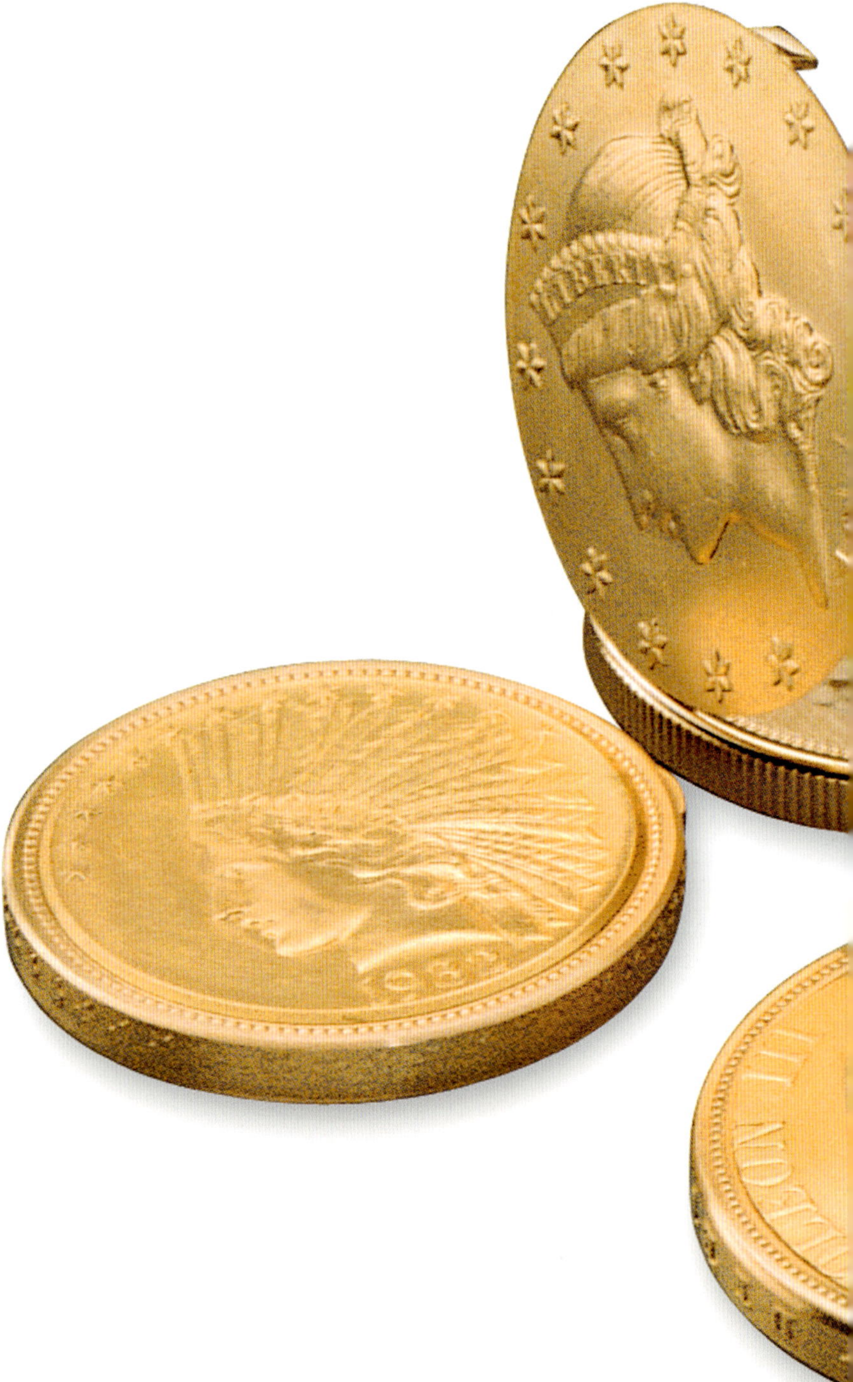

Abundance

Coins
and great minds

Valentin Piaget's creation of ultra-thin movements in the 1950s and at the beginning of the 1960s was an achievement that stimulated the inventiveness of the company's master-watchmakers.

Thus it was that they succeeded in incorporating an entire watch inside the width of a gold coin, without anyone being able to tell if it had been modified or not. A daring gamble that certainly paid off —witness the considerable quantity of these gold-coin watches that were produced and sold.

This achievement drew the attention of the brilliant Salvador Dalí. To satisfy his immense pride, always tinged with self-mockery, he created his own coin. The "Dalí d'Or" came in four different denominations, from the half Dalí to the five Dalí, including one and two Dalí coins, all made from twenty-four-karat gold and minted in limited series. In 1967, he associated with Piaget to create watches and jewellery made from the Dalí d'Or coins—a bold joint venture that was particularly well thought out on the part of Yves G. Piaget and is a good example of the brand's perceptiveness and sensitivity to developing trends. Above all, it shows Yves's qualities as an ambassador who always understood how to forge special connections within the most exclusive and influential circles, even succeeding in convincing the most famous artists to become partners with his company, all the while retaining them as major clients.

The long list of illustrious personalities who designed for Piaget includes, among others, the famous dancer Ludmilla Tchérina and the equally renowned sculptor Arman, who created a series of sculptures in gold and rosewood, inspired by his legendary musical instruments cut into slices.

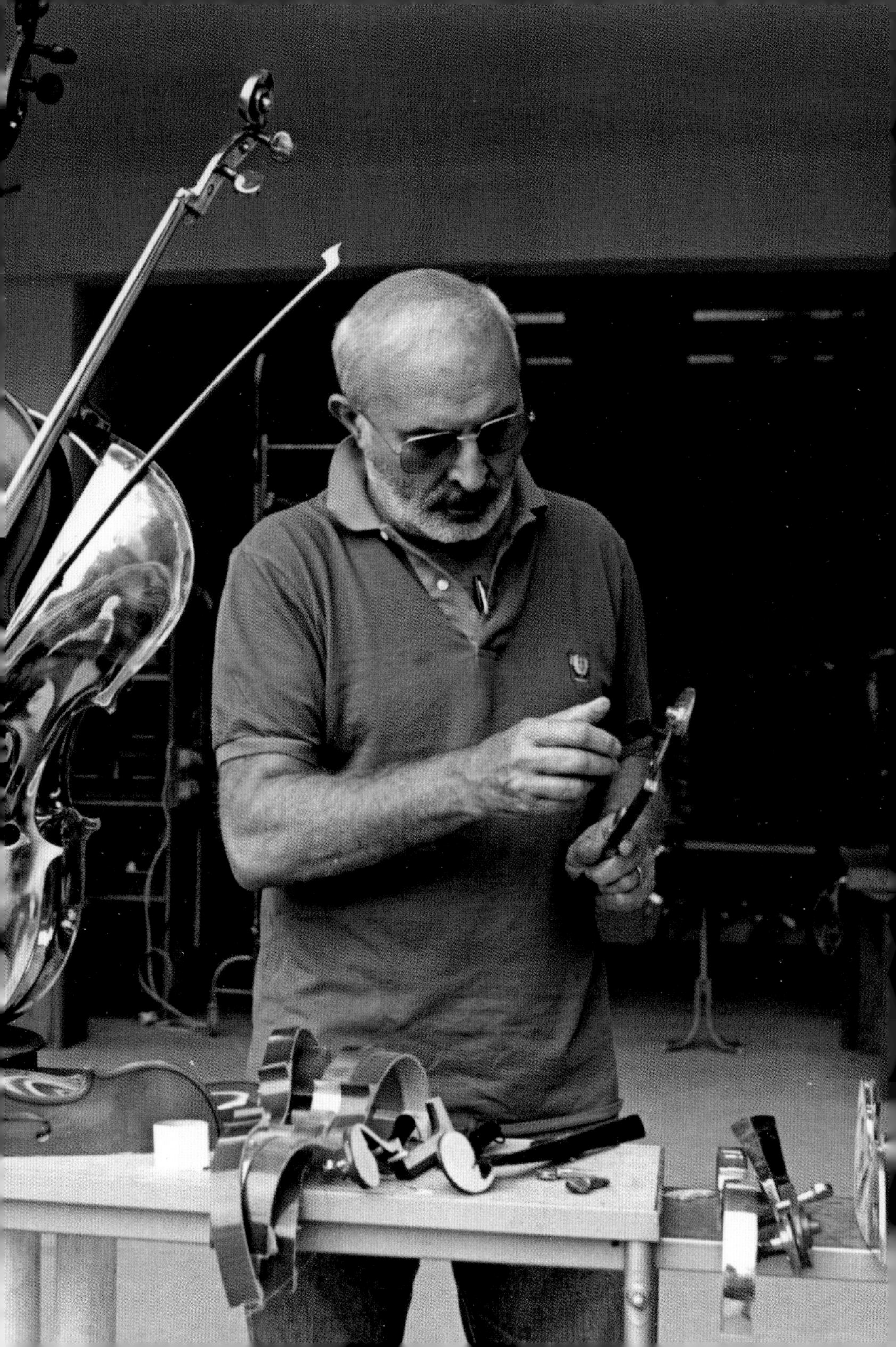

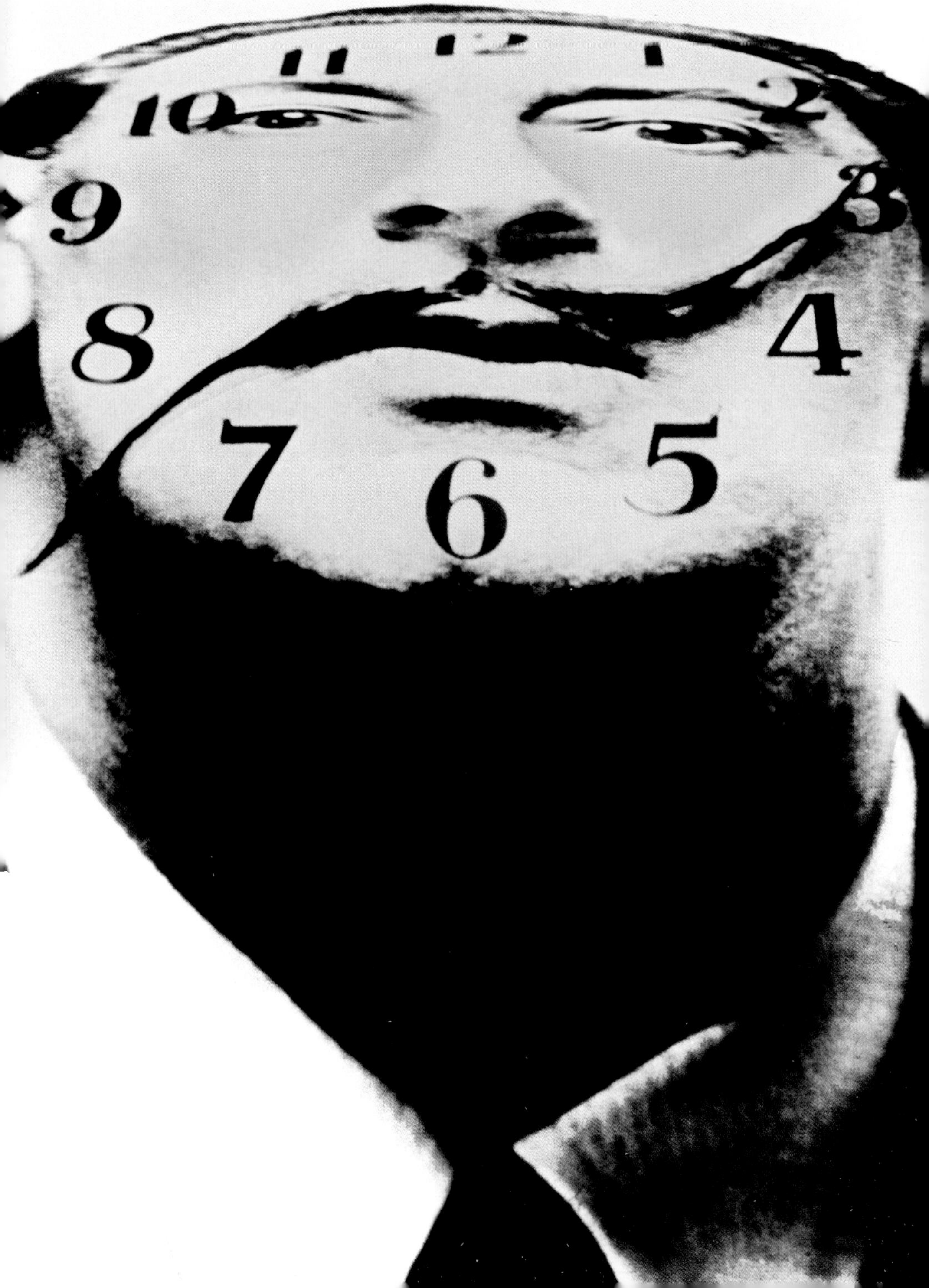

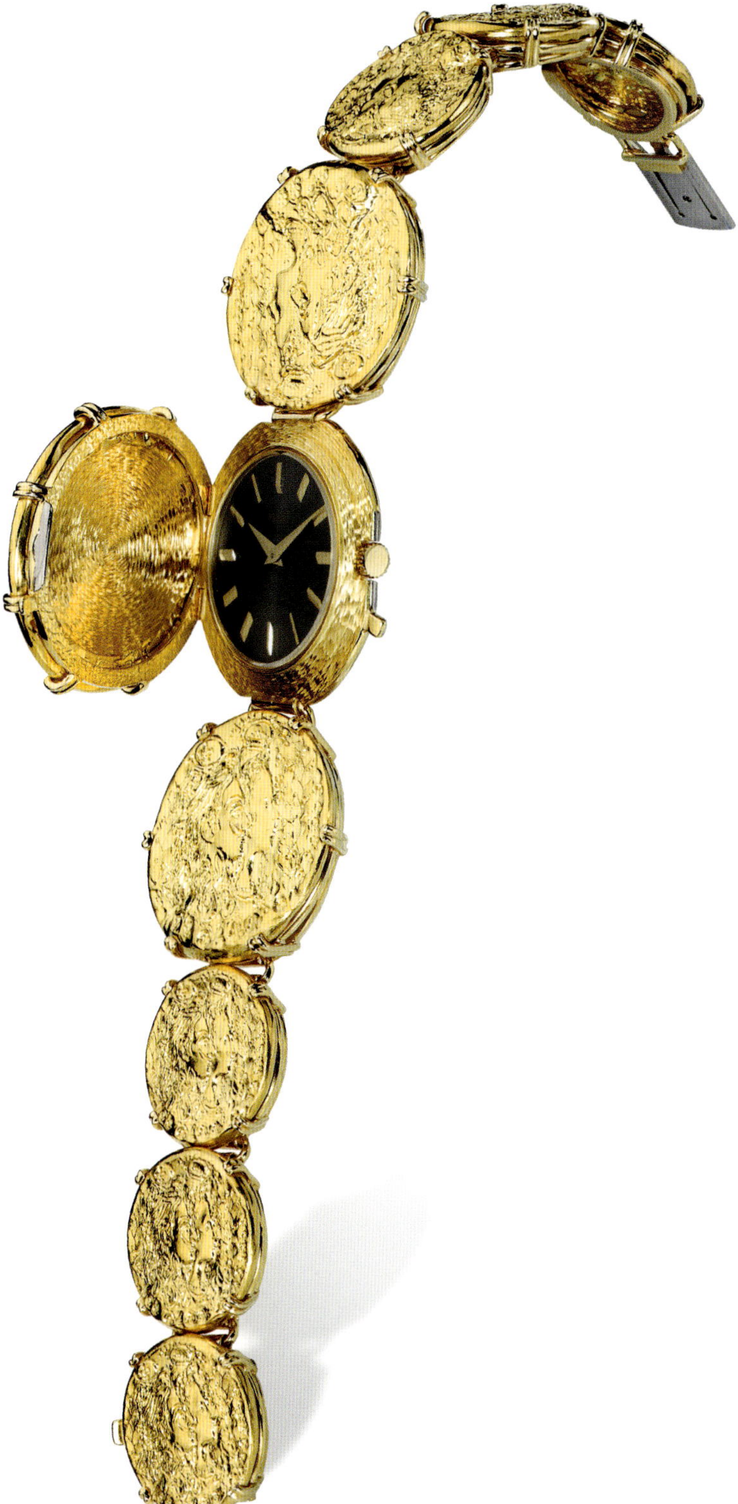

Thanks to friendships maintained by Yves, the name of Piaget was associated with a number of personalities and well-known celebrities of the era: Sammy Davis, Jr., Cary Grant, Gina Lollobrigida, Mireille Mathieu, Liza Minnelli, Roger Moore, Andy Warhol, as well as members of the royal family of Monaco, to name but a few. Piaget became married to art, a resolutely avant-garde union. During this time, the watchmakers and jewellers of La Côte-aux-Fées continued to preserve both quality and continuity—values that were essential if the company wished to endure.

Age-old wisdom and a flair for modernity

The management of the House of Piaget is distinguished by a unique blend of simplicity, insight, and genius. The company's bold expansion during the 1960s and '70s remains an enigma for watchmaking historians, for the company has left no accounting trace, no charts, no statistics, and no year-on-year comparisons of sales figures. The only accurate data were entered in the notebooks of Valentin Piaget who, at the end of each financial year, would show them to other family members. Once they became obsolete, he probably destroyed them.

Throughout this frenzy of expansion, while the brand was opening boutiques in all corners of the world, no one thought to put aside any of the models produced. It was Yves G. Piaget who, during the 1980s, entrusted Emil Keller with the task of buying from individuals or at international auctions some of the most meaningful pieces that had made history—not only for the house, but also for modern watchmaking.

This had been an astonishing oversight on the part of these inhabitants of the Jura valleys steeped in careful traditions, who nonetheless never

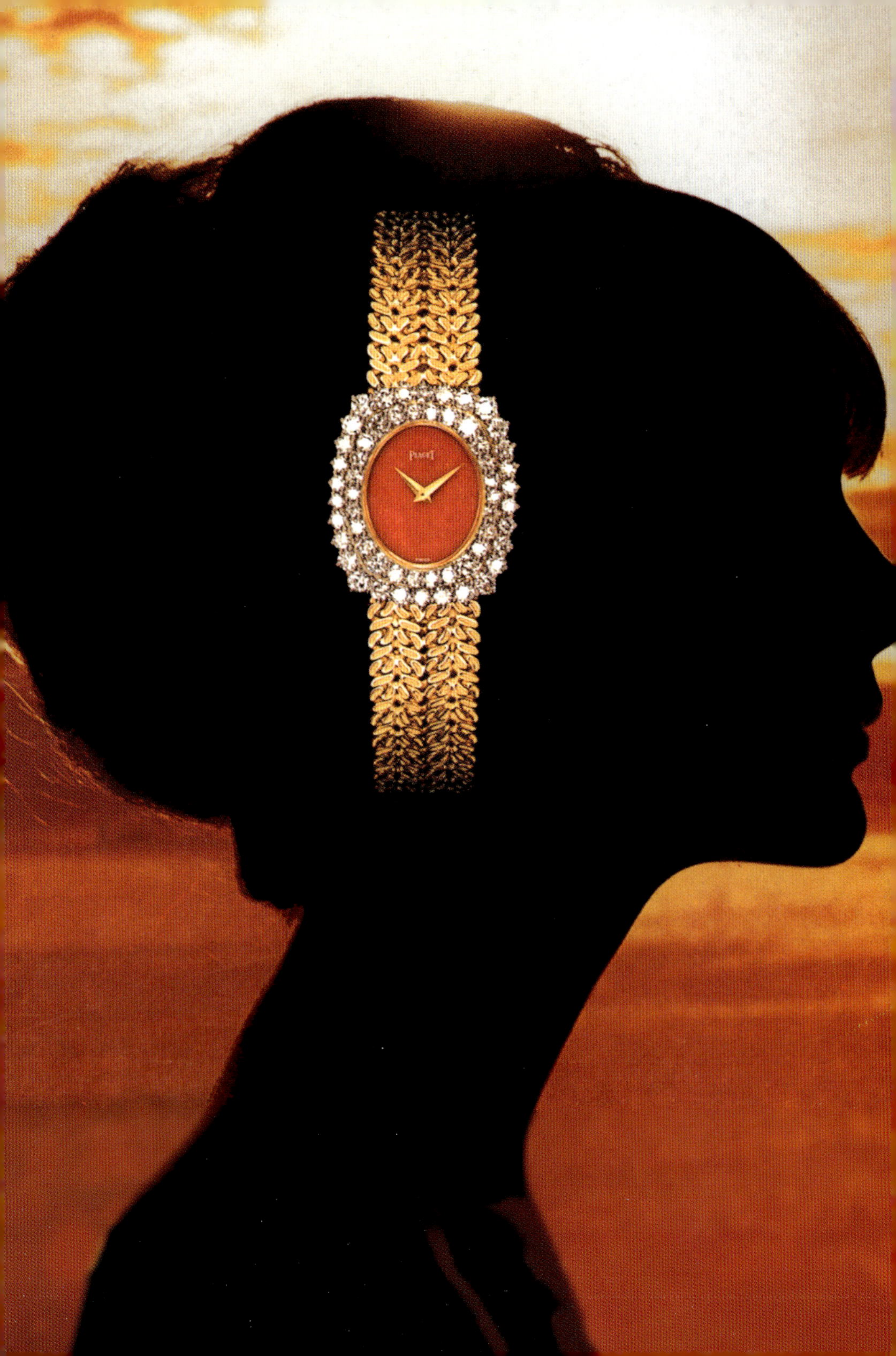
PIAGET

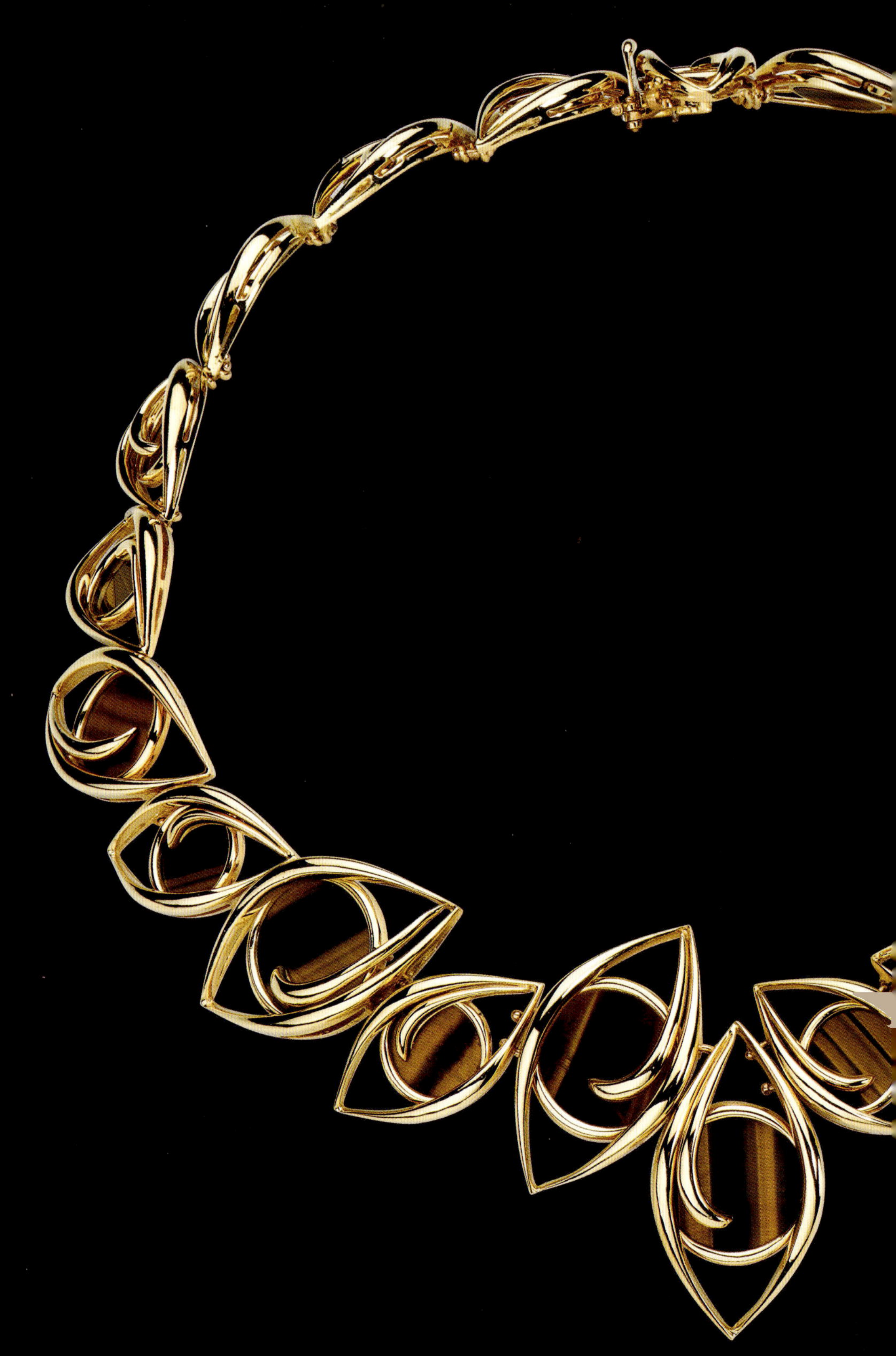

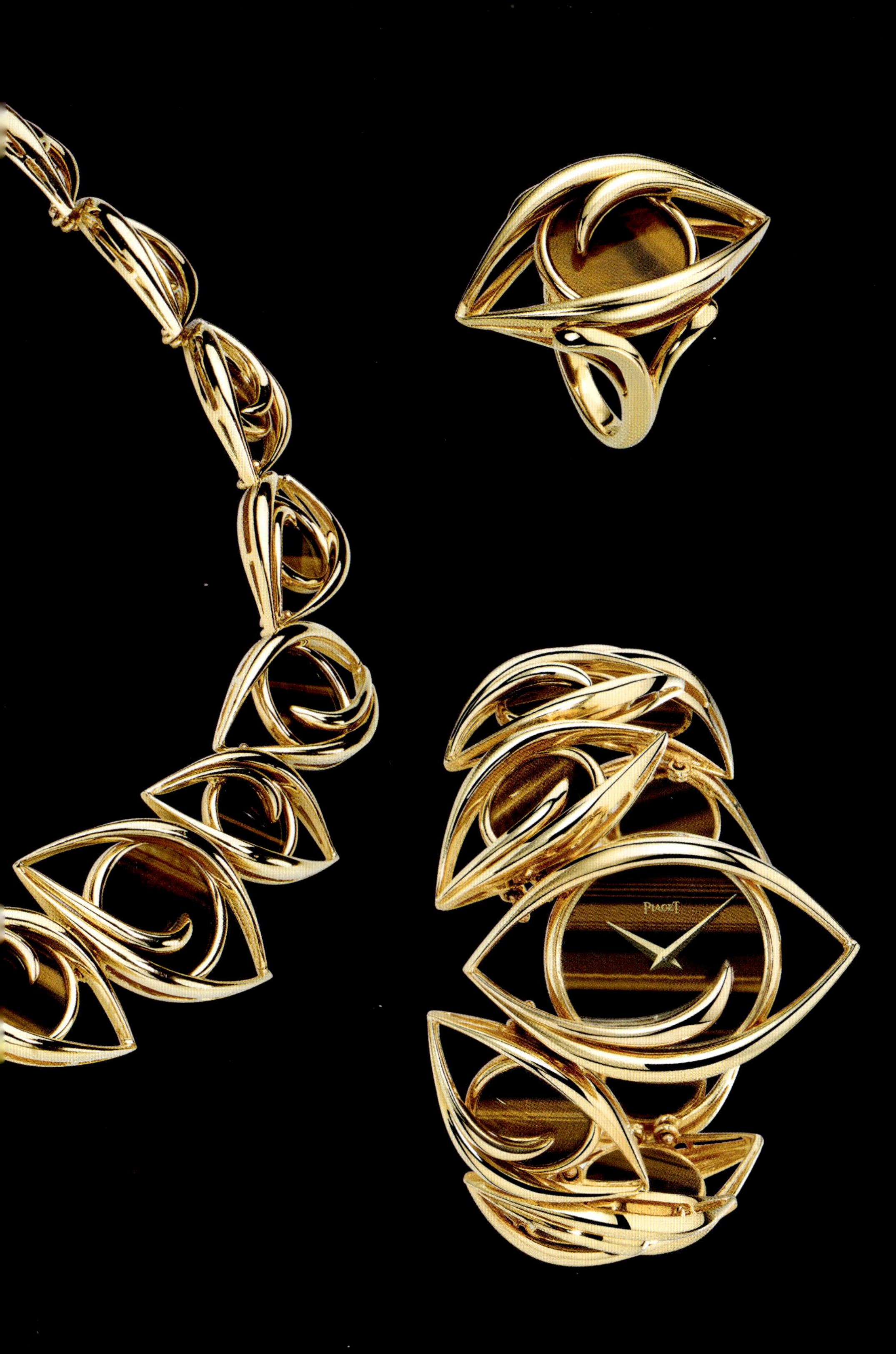
PIAGET

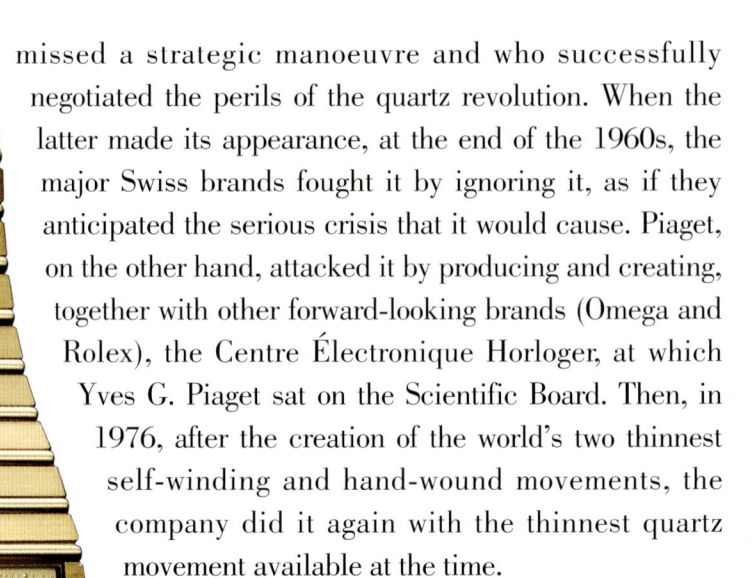

missed a strategic manoeuvre and who successfully negotiated the perils of the quartz revolution. When the latter made its appearance, at the end of the 1960s, the major Swiss brands fought it by ignoring it, as if they anticipated the serious crisis that it would cause. Piaget, on the other hand, attacked it by producing and creating, together with other forward-looking brands (Omega and Rolex), the Centre Électronique Horloger, at which Yves G. Piaget sat on the Scientific Board. Then, in 1976, after the creation of the world's two thinnest self-winding and hand-wound movements, the company did it again with the thinnest quartz movement available at the time.

The "unbeatable" Japanese competition had indeed been surpassed.

The Piaget Polo

In the 1970s, the House of Piaget, urged on by young Yves and his passion for horses, started linking its name to high-society sports events.

For six consecutive years, it sponsored the largest polo tournament in the world: the Piaget World Cup in West Palm Beach, Florida. The company was able to leverage its ties with the sport of kings to promote its new collection of watches, Piaget Polo, which achieved lasting success.

These models enshrined the quintessence of the brand's dual vocation as a watchmaker and a jeweller and achieved perfect equilibrium through a simple and brilliant idea: these square or round watches for men or women would be transformed into a continuous ribbon entirely sculpted from gold and featuring full integration of the dial and bracelet. It would be impossible to say which of the two elements might have been sacrificed. The success of the Piaget Polo watch came specifically from the fact that each part was in fact enhanced by its intimate relationship with the other.

At the end of the 1980s, Piaget remembered that the horse is man's most noble conquest and observed that thoroughbreds are raised for their beauty and their performances—exactly the same values embodied in Piaget watches.

The brand reaffirmed its ties with the equestrian world by generously sponsoring the Deauville Gold Cup, one of the best-attended society sporting events. It then extended its approach by sponsoring the Piaget Gold Cup of the Hong Kong Jockey Club, an event that entranced more than sixty thousand spectators in a single evening.

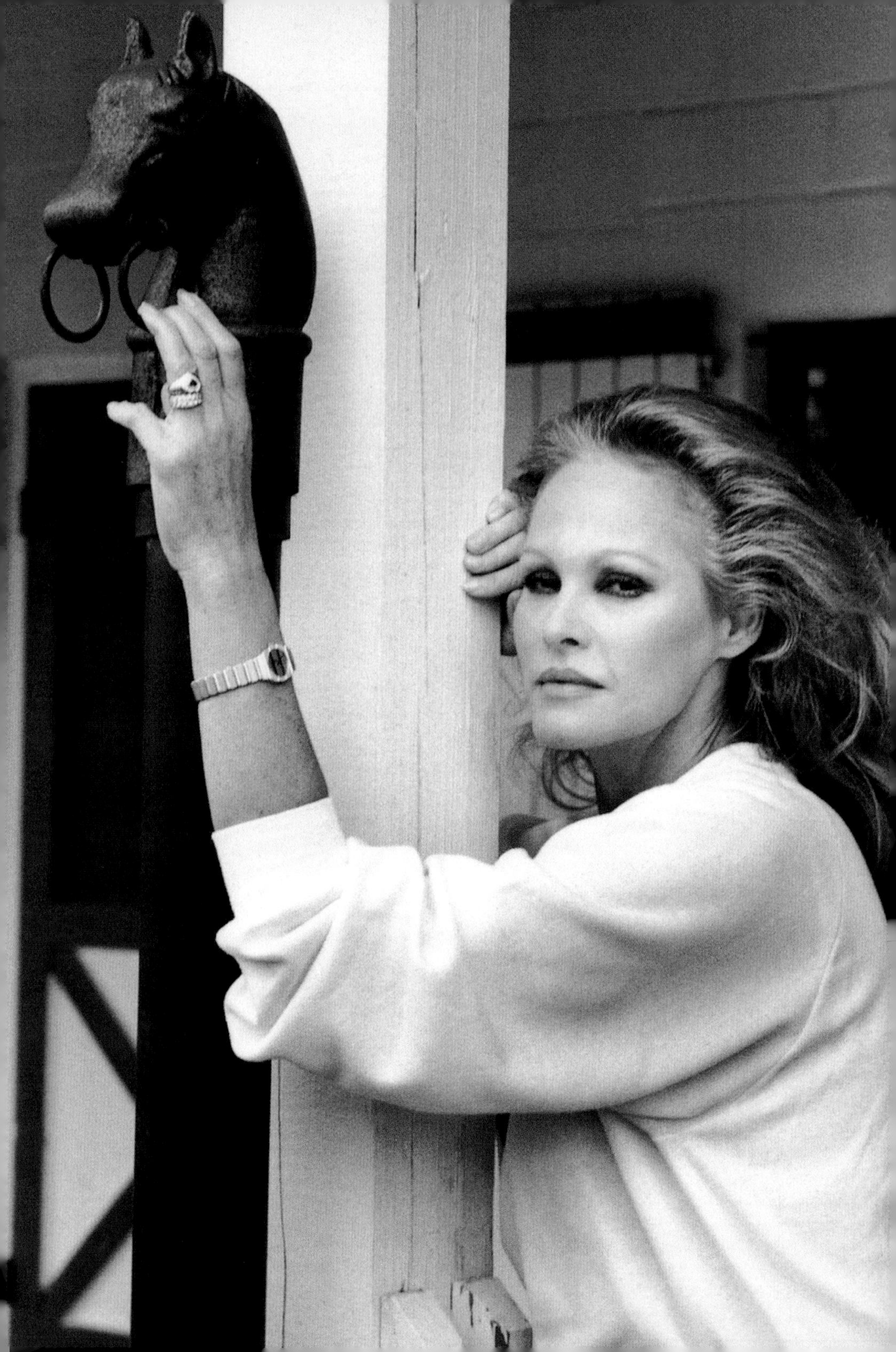

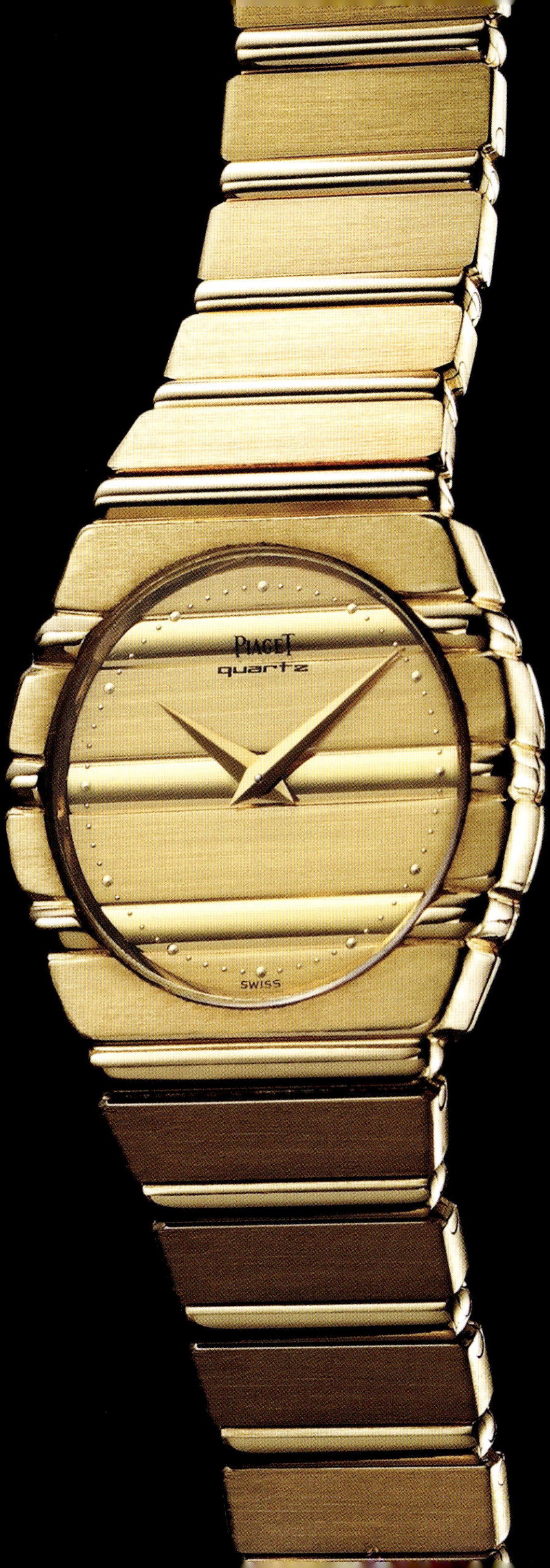
PIAGET
quartz
SWISS

The name of the rose

Yves G. Piaget cultivated a number of passions that fostered the harmonious development of the brand within a field that had hitherto been the exclusive preserve of a few great Parisian names. Among them is one for which the verb "cultivate" is especially appropriate: his love of flowers, and of roses, in particular. Since 1976, he has been one of the judges of the International New Rose Contest, which is held each year in Geneva. It was his idea to promote this show by presenting the winner with a gold rose created in the Piaget workshops in Geneva.

The first time the prize was awarded, in 1978, it generated so much enthusiasm that the trophy was described in these extravagant terms: "It is a life-size solid-gold rose signed by Piaget. Surely there is no other prize in the world of floriculture more coveted than this: the Gold Rose of Geneva."

At the start of the 1980s, the well-known horticulturalist Alain Meilland dedicated a rose that he had created to Yves G. Piaget. The flower had twenty-four dentate petals, pale coloring, and a sweet perfume. In a remarkable turn of events, it won the highest prize at the Geneva contest in 1982.

Naturally, this rose became the emblematic jewelled motif of the brand for the "Magic Gardens of Piaget" collection.

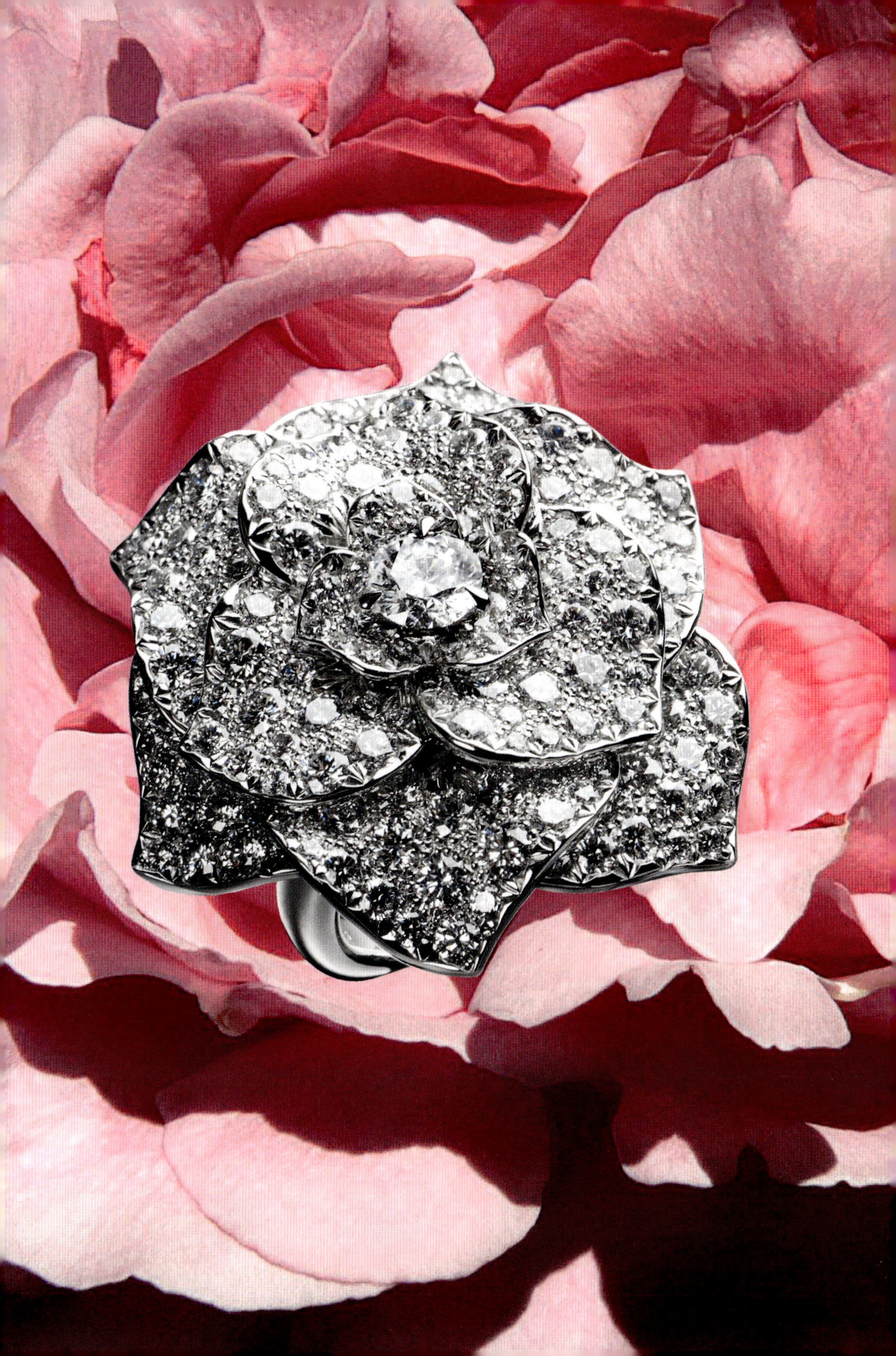

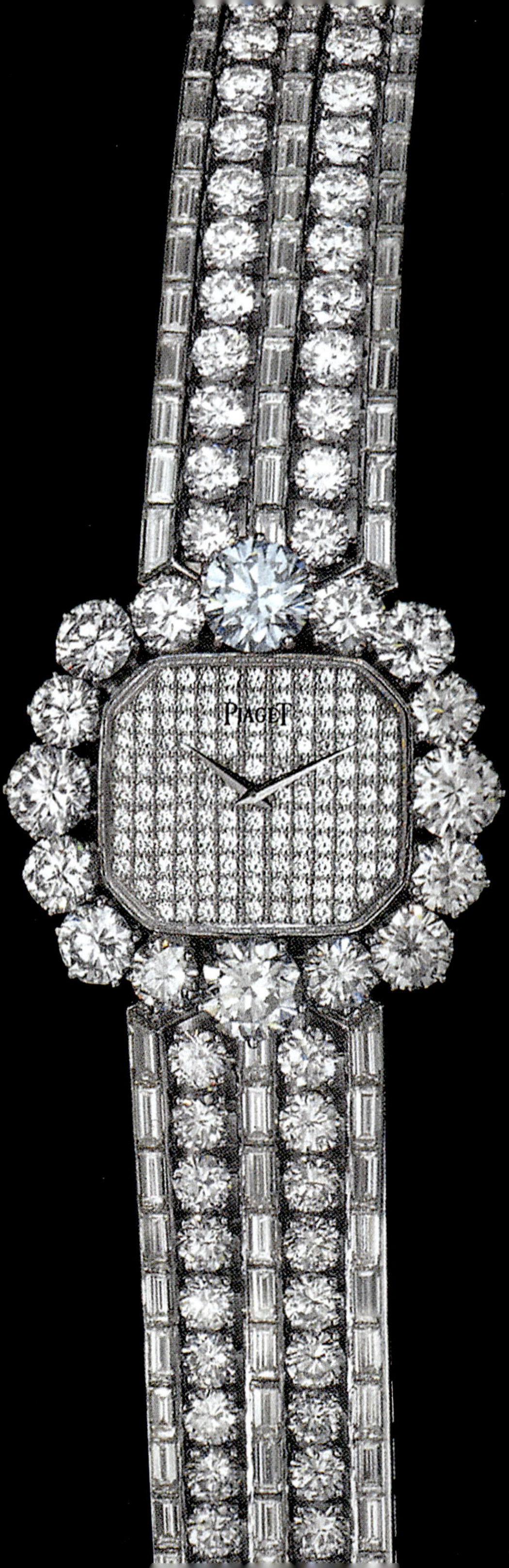
PIAGET

The Piaget follies

Piaget was well prepared for the flashy, frivolous decade of the 1980s, a time when luxury and hedonism triumphed. In 1982, as new trends began to emerge, Piaget, having consistently set new technical records for more than twenty years, began to explore another area: the creation of the most expensive men's watch of the time. Made of 154 grams of platinum, the "Phoebus" was set with 269 of the purest diamonds, totalling 87.87 karats. Among them sat enthroned a 3.85-karat blue diamond of unparalleled lustre. Ordered by a rich Japanese client, it cost 3.5 million Swiss francs and required two years of work by the house's master jewellers. It was first displayed at the prestigious Red Cross Gala in Monaco, where Sylvia Kristel appeared alongside Yves G. Piaget, who was now recognized as the house's official ambassador.

The Japanese collector who bought this exceptional piece for himself was not the only wealthy aesthete to favor the brand.

Piaget was famous for its ability to fulfill the most extravagant desires. The American pianist Liberace proudly sported a piano-shaped watch created by Piaget, featuring a sapphire-and-diamond keyboard. He had another version made in mother-of-pearl and onyx. The French thriller writer Frédéric Dard, the creator of the San Antonio series, owned a Piaget watch shaped like a book, with a black face and the word "Minuit"—a reference to the Editions de Minuit publishing house—engraved along with his name on the upper edge of the case.

Gina Lollobrigida, when visiting Cuba, received a curious proposal from Fidel Castro: to exchange her diamond-studded Piaget watch for the watch worn in battle by the Lider Maximo. She readily agreed.

From the classic to the contemporary, from exuberance to extravagance, Piaget's creativity anticipated the spirit of the era.

A new dimension

On the threshold of the 1990s, the company, while financially very sound and still riding the crest of the wave, nevertheless decided that the family business structure, until then jealously safeguarded, was no longer sufficient to guarantee its expansion.
Throughout the world, and especially in the luxury sector, companies and brand names were in the throes of ever greater concentration within powerful international conglomerates. But the Piagets had abided by family traditions, particularly that of never owing anything to banks. Every investment made by a bank was self-financed. However, this type of management was not flexible enough to adapt to the inevitable changes that were to occur.
The fact that the Piagets grasped this in due time was further proof of the dynasty's characteristic clear-sightedness. Therefore, on April 26, 1988, in a press conference that caused a considerable stir in the media, Cartier officially announced its acquisition of the Piaget and Baume & Mercier brands. The news was simultaneously broadcast via satellite to Paris, Brussels, Geneva, London, Madrid, Milan, and Munich—an unusual audiovisual feat for the time and proof of Piaget's exceptional innovative powers.

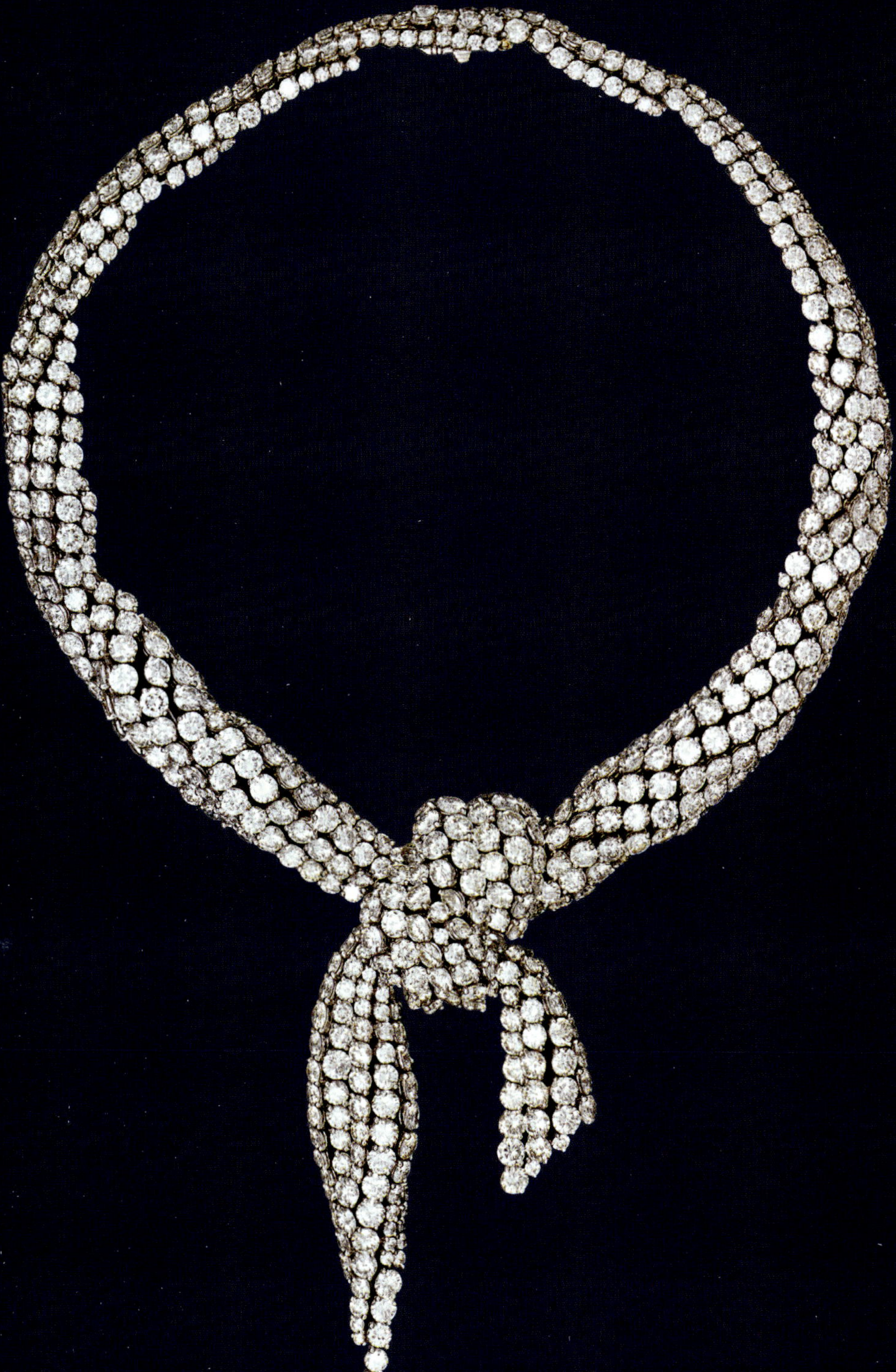

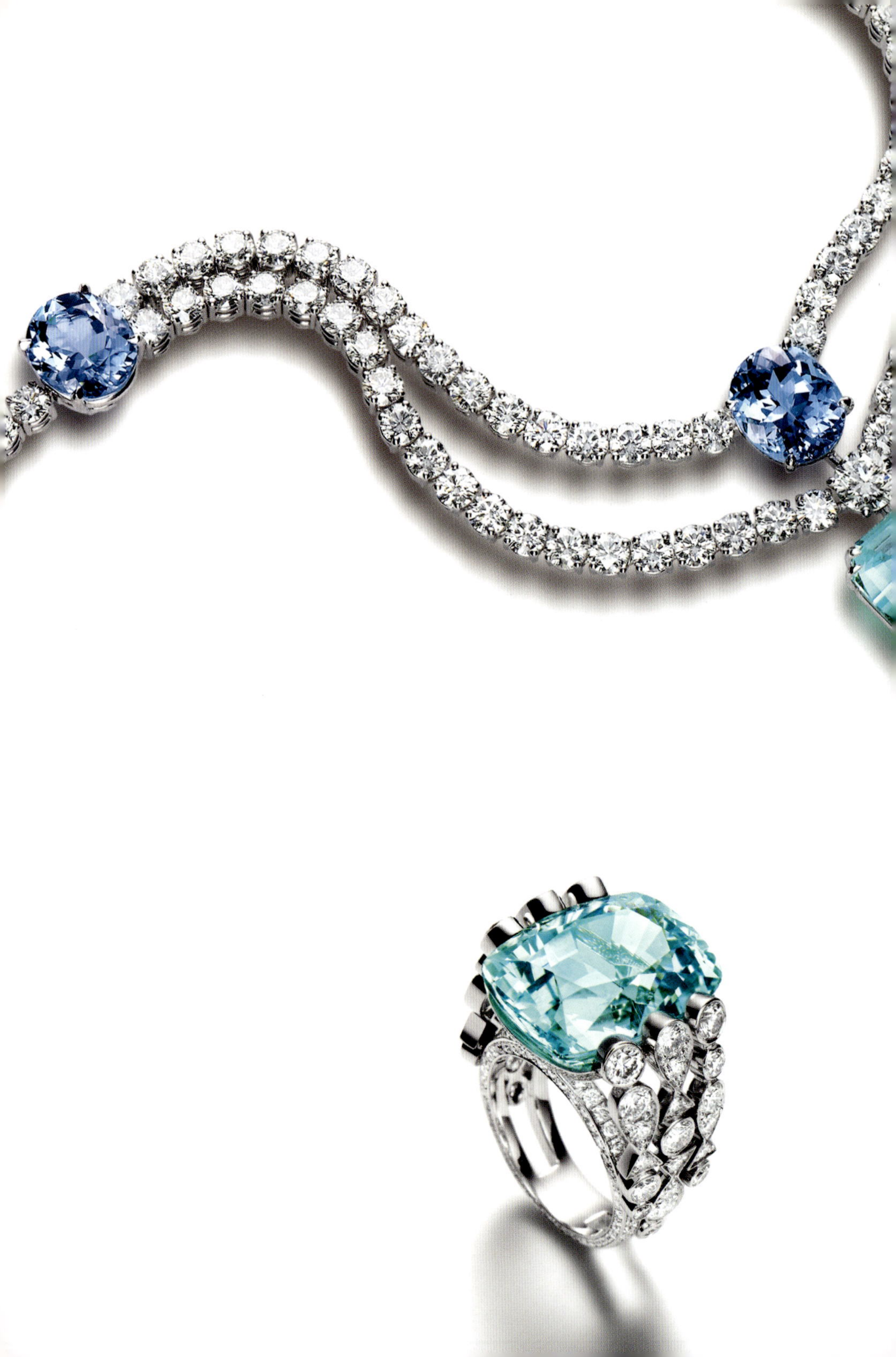

Splendours

The marvels of Geneva and the marvels of Piaget

In the early 1990s, Piaget offered its admirers the opportunity to discover a half century of masterpieces of its production with the *Montres et Merveilles* ("Watches and Wonders"), exhibition, a selection of pieces from the collection being constituted by Yves G. Piaget and Emil Keller.

Montres et Merveilles was first presented in Milan in 1992 at the sumptuous Palazzo Reale, before being shown in 1994 in Geneva's Museum of Watchmaking and Enamelwork. The public was thus able to view the watches that had forged Piaget's reputation, as well as high-quality enamelled jewellery—an art that had contributed to Geneva's worldwide fame.

By combining these two facets of its personality, Piaget was celebrating its love for the city of Calvin as well as highlighting its twin vocation as both a watchmaker and a jeweller. The exhibition displayed the art of Piaget as the culmination of a process that had been jointly fueled by tradition and creative strength.

Creative abundance

Throughout the 1990s, Piaget's stature as the jeweller of movement was asserted through another line of emblematic jewellery bearing the evocative name "Possession."

The originality of the "Possession" line lies in a simple yet brilliant idea which was an integral part of its design: two inextricably entwined gold bands turning freely around each other, evoking perpetual movement. They convey a symbolic message: the ring is the symbol of the love that forever joins two individuals, all the while preserving their individual personalities and freedom.

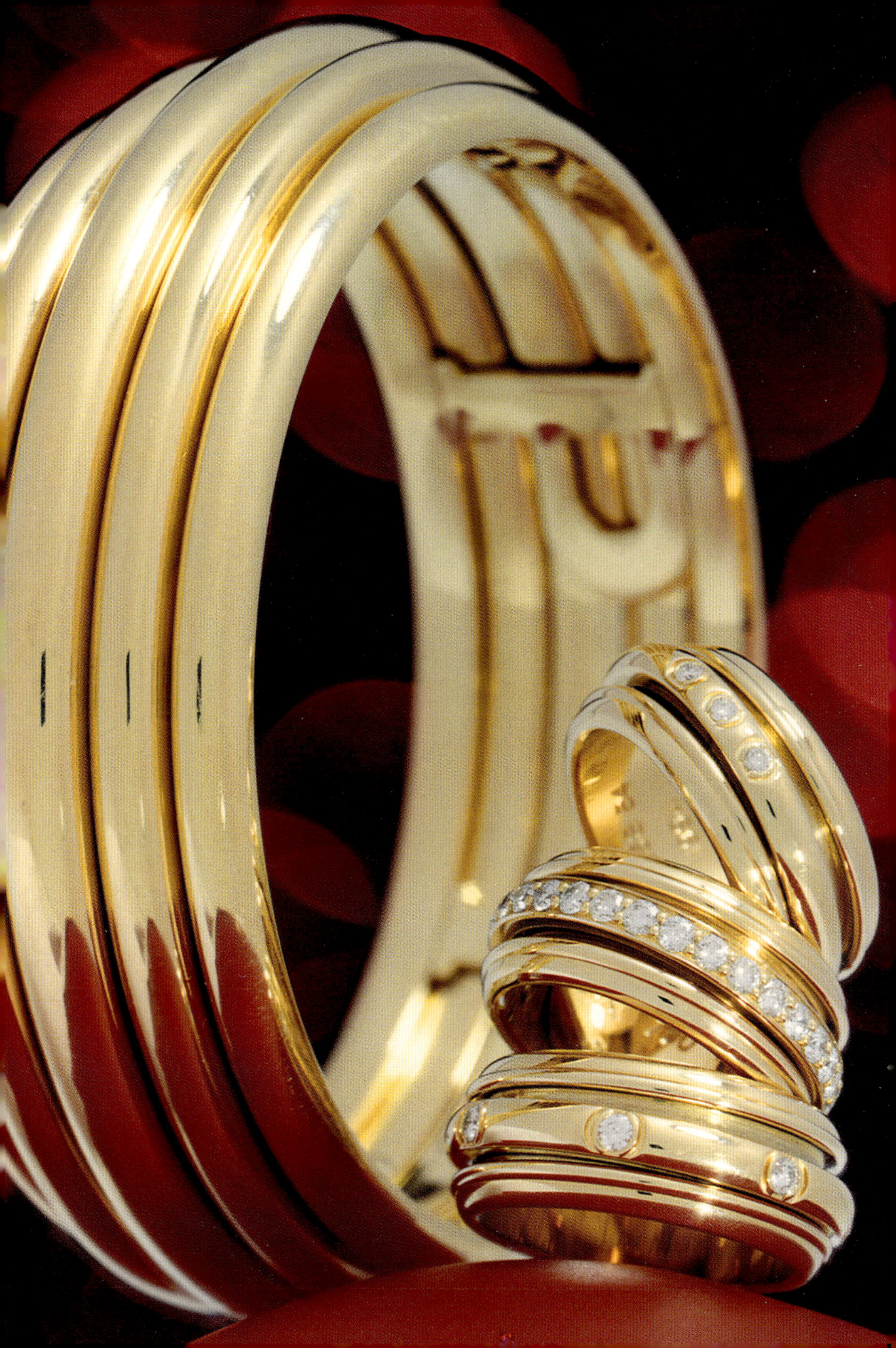

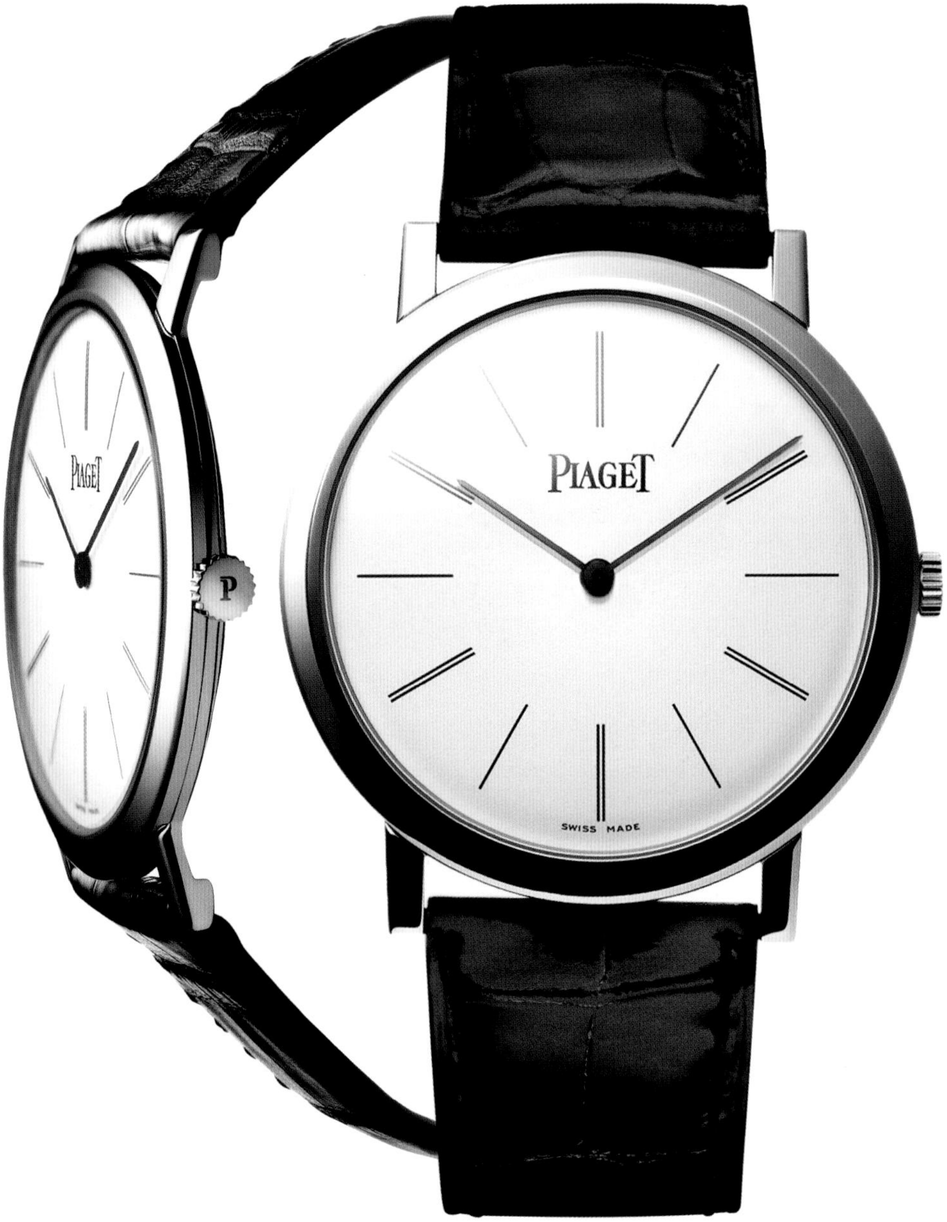
PIAGET
P
PIAGET
SWISS MADE

"Possession" wins people's hearts through its playful dimension and its creativity. Constantly reborn in new variations, this collection has become a classic that caught the attention of the French star of American basketball, Tony Parker, and his wife, the actress Eva Longoria Parker, who exchanged "Possession" rings when they married, on July 7, 2007.

Ever curious and ready to explore new avenues, at the approach of the millennium, Piaget launched a boldly contemporary new collection inspired by Hollywood glamour: "Limelight".

Its jewellery creations were based on a dual approach, combining the sparkle of diamonds with extreme formal purity. These were generously sized, mid- and high-range pieces with broad diamond-set surfaces reminiscent of the popping flashbulbs and dazzling footlights that inspired the name of the collection.

This overview would not be complete without Piaget's famous interpretation of the heart—a timeless jewellery best-seller.

At the same time, the *manufacture* continued to innovate with new movement lines: the 430P and the 500P. It launched the collection of ultra-thin "Piaget Altiplano" watches, symbols of purity and timeless elegance.

Recognition in Venice

In confirmation of its ever greater and more flattering international prestige, Piaget was commissioned by the City of Venice to restore the Piazza San Marco Clock Tower to its former splendour and to perfect working order. One of the world's oldest and most famous clocks, it was built in 1499 by two artisans from Reggio nell'Emilia, Rainieri and Son. On February 1, 1999, its five-hundredth anniversary, the clock's mechanism was presented, entirely restored.

To celebrate this success, Piaget created an exceptional new watch: a skeleton chronograph in the colours of Venice. Seven years later, the tower itself was finally restored and once again the clock rang out on the Piazza San Marco, during a celebration that included Piaget. As a fitting commemoration of this internationally significant event, Piaget's watchmakers created another exceptional watch: the "Piaget Polo Tourbillon Relatif" —a one-of-a-kind model in blue-and-white enamel, featuring a dial design echoing the stylistic features of the San Marco clock.

A new *manufacture* for the future

Determined to establish its place firmly in the new century, the company inaugurated its new Manufacture de Haute Horlogerie on the outskirts of Geneva. It is an outstanding facility uniting forty watchmaking and jewellery divisions and serving as a complement to the production of watch movements in La Côte-aux-Fées. This effective integration has enabled Piaget to create twenty-one exclusive movements during the past decade.

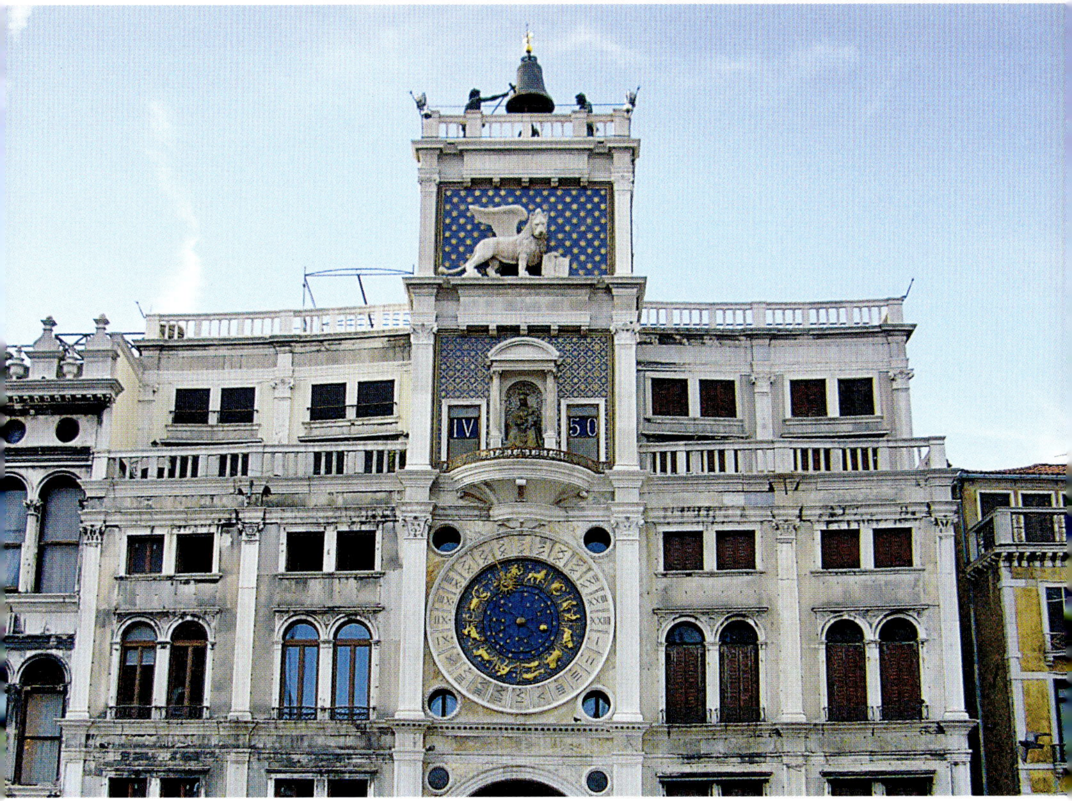
IV
50

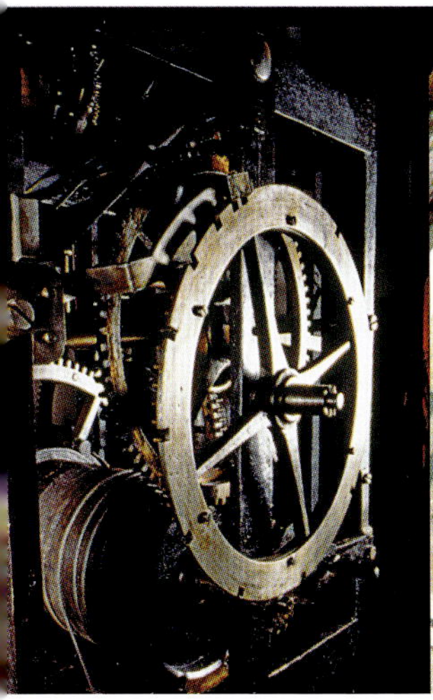

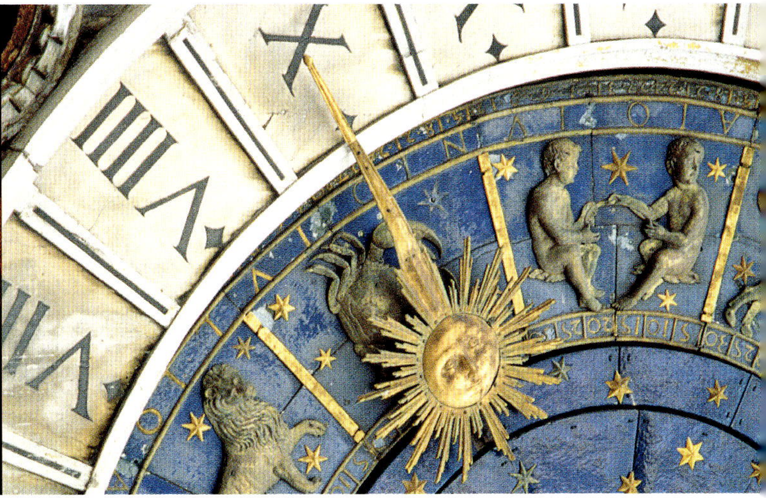

This is an amazing feat in itself, even more so because of the highly complex structures of some of these movements: Calibre 600P, the thinnest tourbillion movement in the world, at just 3.5 millimetres thick; Calibre 608P, with its spectacular tourbillion *relatif* movement; Calibre 880P, with a flyback chronograph movement and a dual time-zone display; and Calibre 885P, with a perpetual calendar, to name but a few.

Having the designers, the master watchmakers, and the master jewellers under the same roof enables the house to explore uncharted territory. The "Limelight Magic Hour" watch is a perfect illustration of this: a playful, unique watch that can take on different forms, with a bezel that pivots in three positions to reveal or hide the gold, diamond-set numerals on the dial, which remains fixed. Truly an act of magic. Piaget's integrated manufacturing expertise has also enabled the company to present new, exquisitely creative high-end jewellery collections each year, despite tight development schedules.

3,5 mm

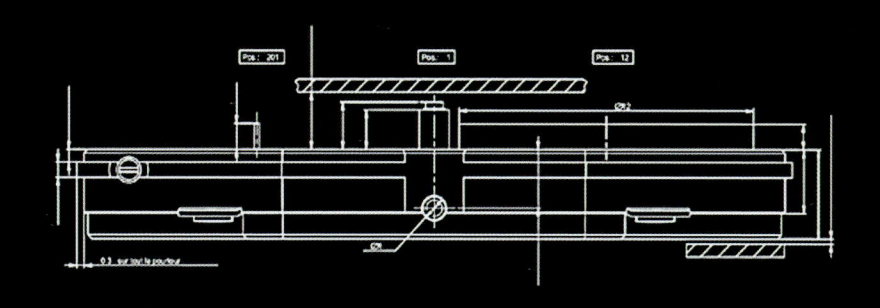

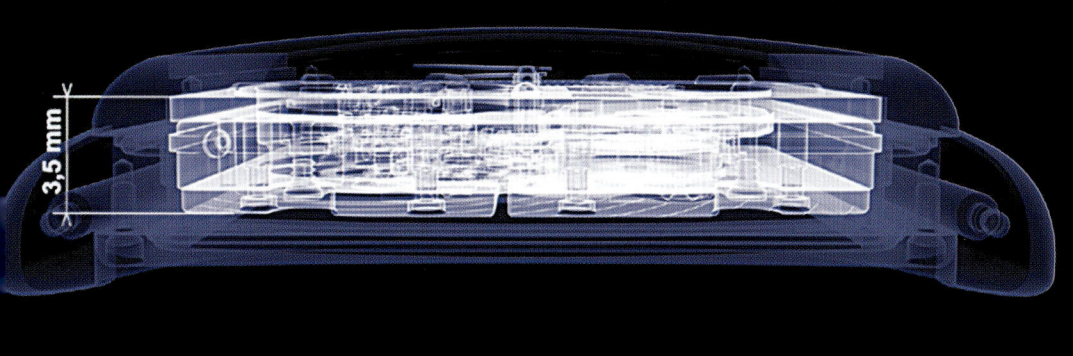

Boundless creativity

Since 2003, Piaget has regularly introduced themed collections of *haute joaillerie*. Buoyed by an advertising campaign that shows the products in French gardens, Piaget explores the poetic universe of nature. It is a nature that is domesticated, designed, and structured by the human hands that sculpt the magical gardens from which the house's creators draw their inspiration and create collections with motifs of roses, fountains and droplets, leaves and topiaries.

To highlight the brand's extravagant creativity, the internationally known contemporary French artists Pierre & Gilles worked with the house on a remarkable marketing campaign in 2005. In a series of painted photographs, each of which is one-of-a-kind, they created timeless portraits suffused with love and grace. The colourful, fantastic universe of Pierre & Gilles conjured up dreams of a glamorous, seductive woman and provided Piaget's most beautiful collections with a flamboyant mode of expression.

Inspired by this momentum, Piaget has moved on from the world of the garden to the world of celebration, ever present in the brand's spirit since the 1980s. This festive mood is reinvented annually in the "Limelight" collection. Champagne bubbles in yellow sapphire, diamond lacework, gold sequins, and onyx discs offer a festive evocation of the jet-setting worlds of New York and Paris, of tropical islands, and of jazz nights. These creations highlight the boldness, extravagance, and creativity of Piaget.

In the same glamorous spirit, a number of Hollywood celebrities now join Piaget each year in celebrating with the company the Spirit Awards, for which an annual ceremony is held in Los Angeles, to reward the best achievements in independent cinema in North America. Piaget has supported this event since 2008 and unveils its latest creations on this occasion.

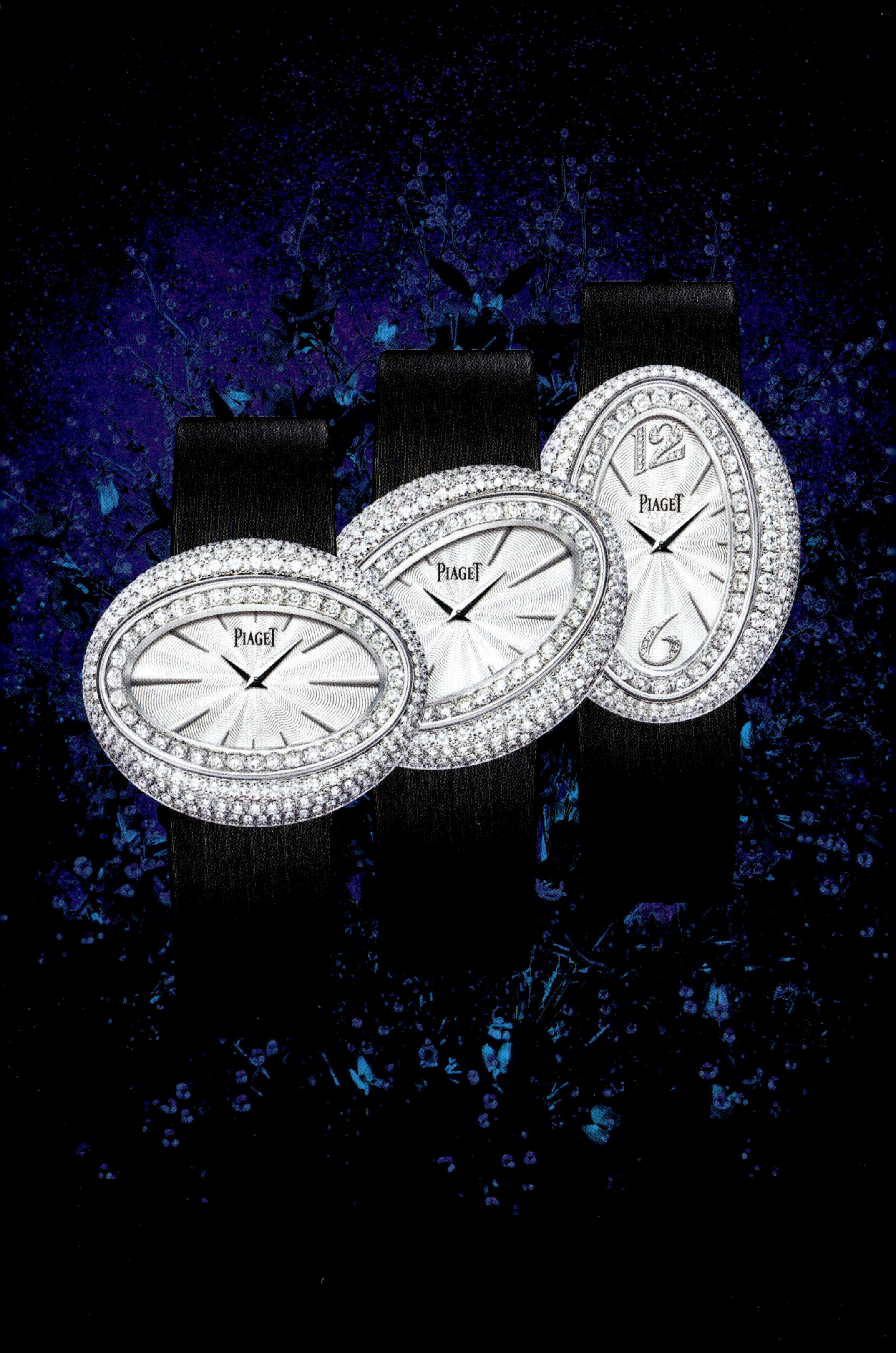
PIAGET
PIAGET
PIAGET

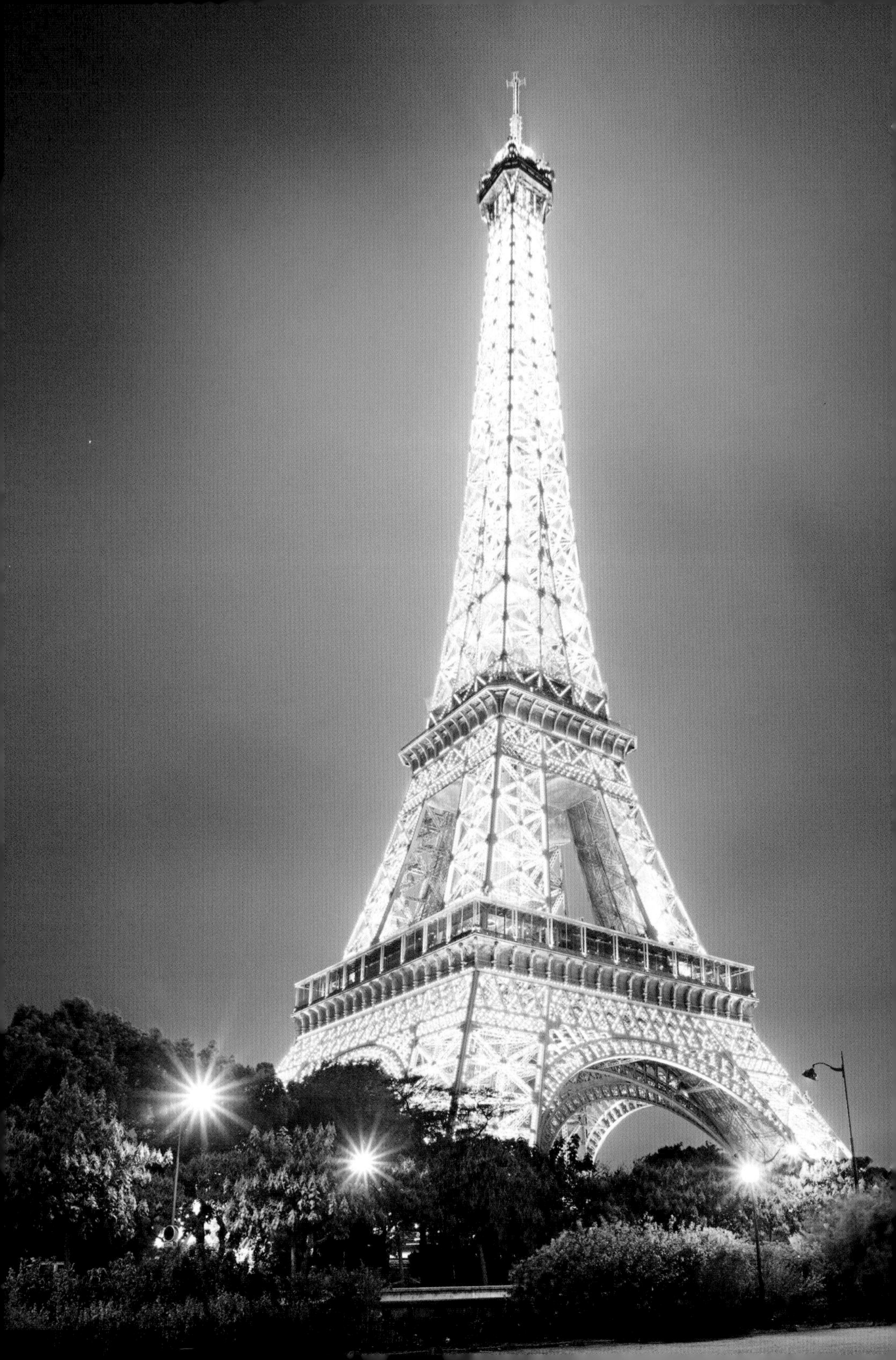

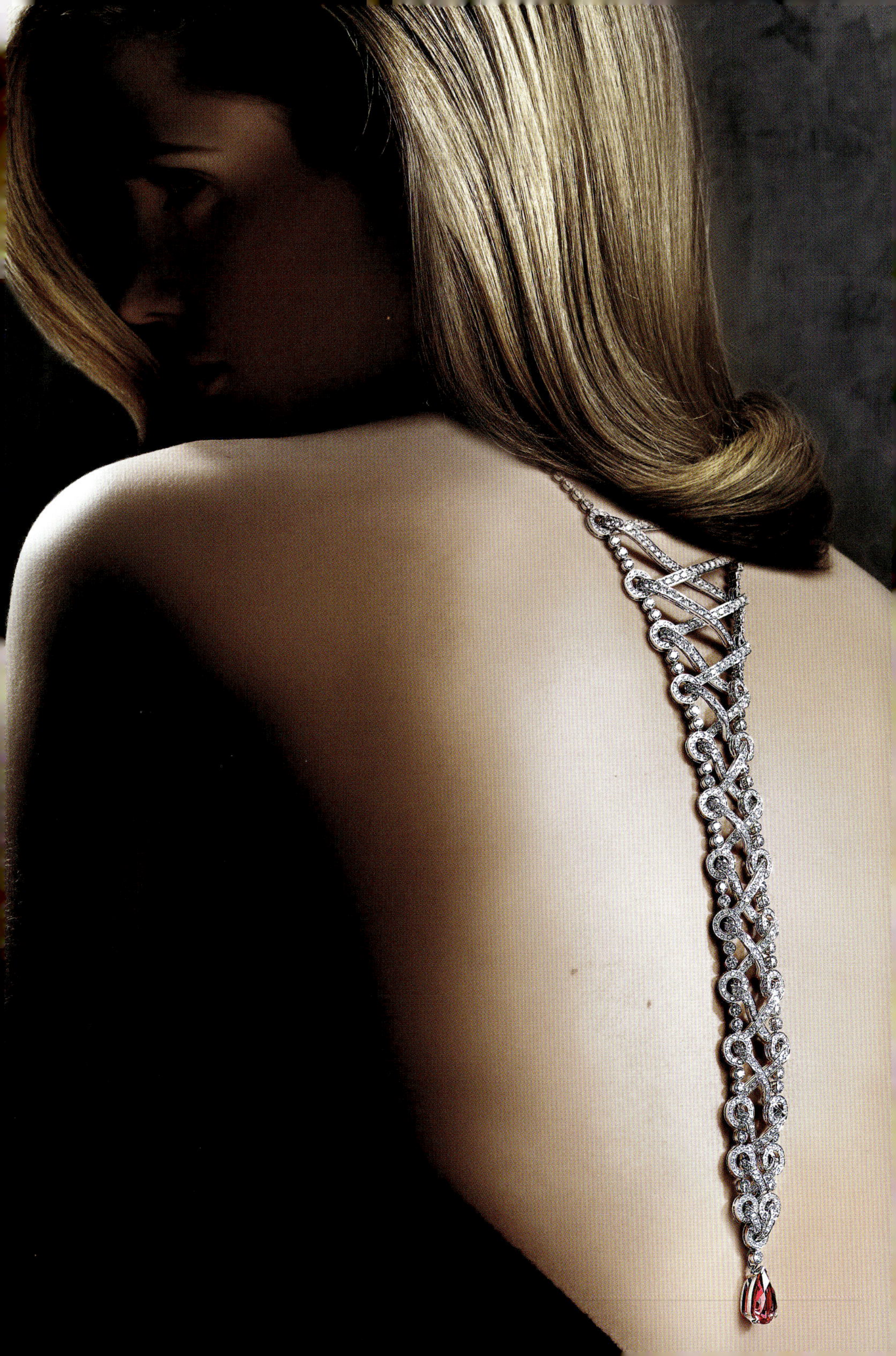

Always do better than necessary

For more than 135 years, Piaget's sole desire has been to marry exemplary technique with inimitable style, while remaining consistently ahead of its time. Expertise, creation, innovation, and excellence are expressed each year in its new releases. In 2010, the "Possession" collection celebrates twenty-five years of success with a new family of self-winding ultra-thin calibres in a tribute to the fiftieth anniversary of the legendary 12P movement.

At just 2.35 millimetres thick, the new 1208P movement is the thinnest self-winding calibre on the market and a perfect illustration of Piaget's motto: *Toujours faire mieux que nécessaire.* (Always do better than necessary.)

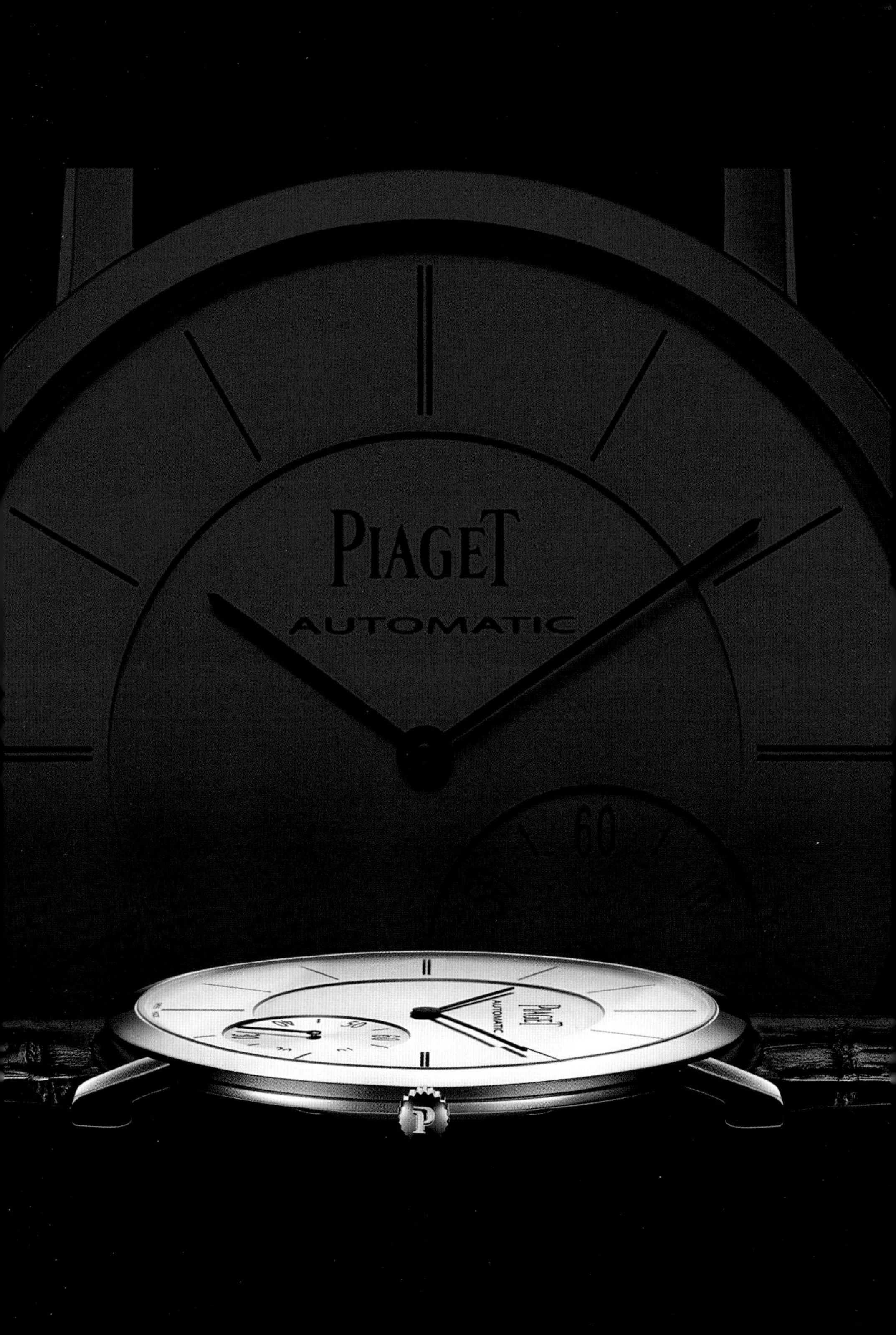
PIAGET
AUTOMATIC
60

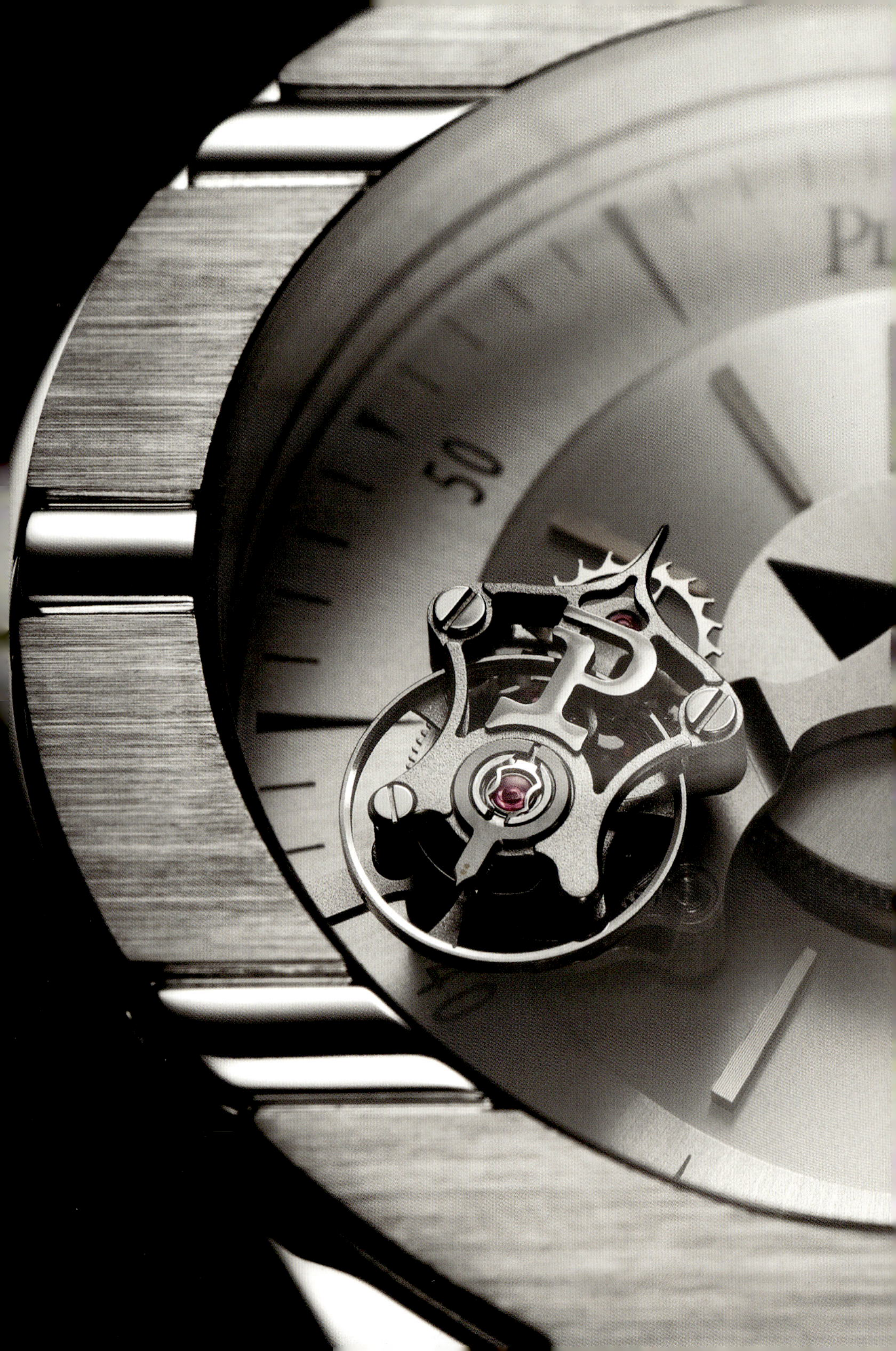

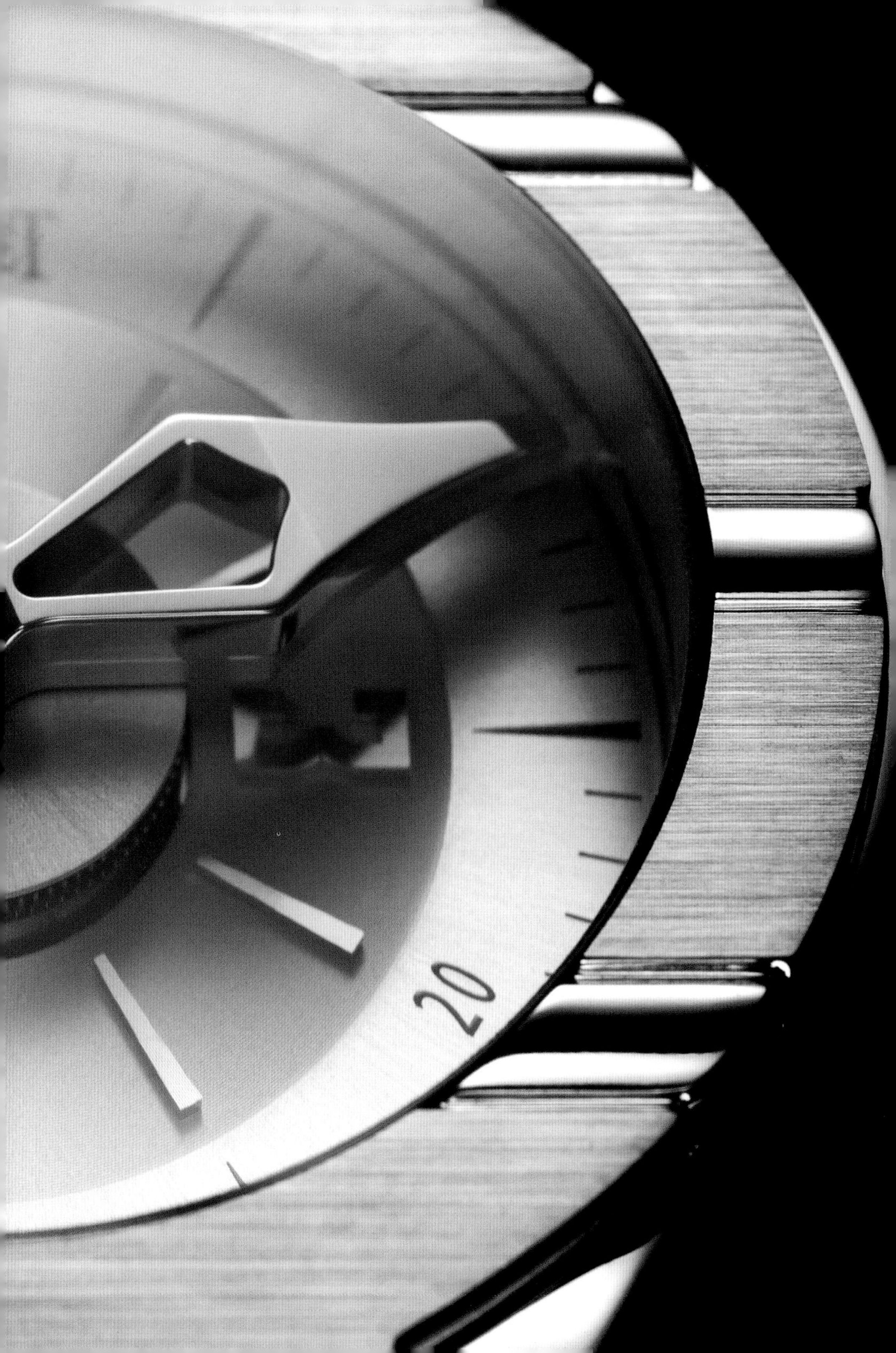
20

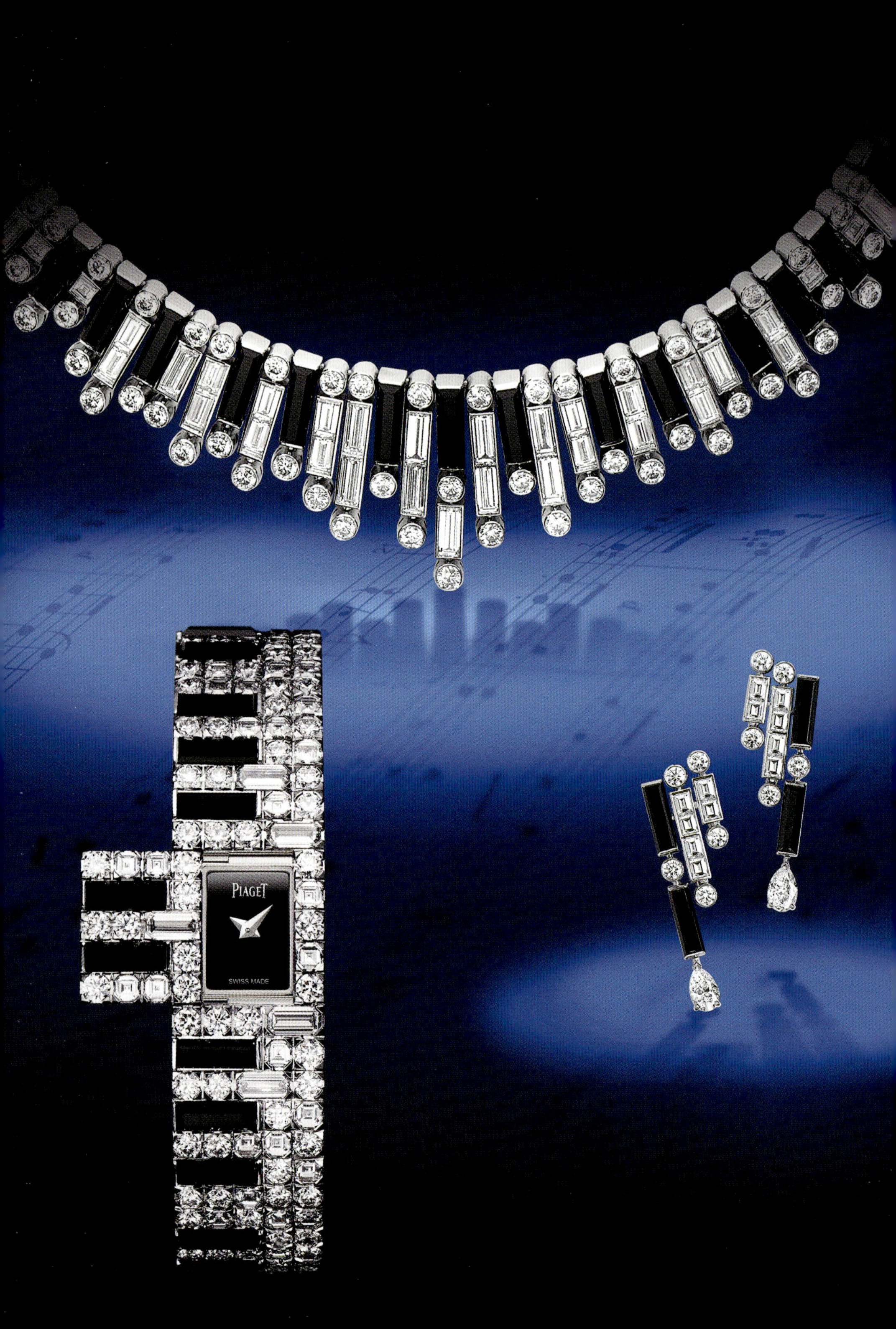
PIAGET
SWISS MADE

Chronology

1874: At the age of nineteen, Georges Edouard Piaget (1855-1931) founds the House which still bears his name today, in La Côte-aux-Fées, a village in the Swiss Canton Jura. After apprenticing as a watchmaker, he joins his family in their work for various watch manufacturers.

1890: The workshop moves from the family farm to the ground floor of the chapel of the Free Evangelical Church of La Côte-aux-Fées.

1911: Timothée Piaget, one of the founder's sons, becomes head of the company. It becomes a partnership company and begins to supply the top watch brands.

1925-1928: Piaget manufactures high-quality, ultra-thin watch movements.

Circa 1930: Piaget begins to supply movements to Longines-Wittnauer (Canada/United States) on a regular basis.

1943: The Piaget trademark is registered.

1945: Gérald Piaget becomes president and managing director of the company, assisted by his brother Valentin who is in charge of the technical and technological development of the movements produced by the House as well as design (cuffs, chains, etc.).
Construction of the main building of the present-day facility in La Côte-aux-Fées.
A specific entity manufactures movements for a few prestigious brands and for a still very limited number of watches that bear the Piaget brand name.

1946: Piaget participates in the Basel Watch Fair for the first time.

1952: Creation of Calibre 2P (21,600 alternations/hour).

1957: Launch of Calibre 9P (19,800 alternations/hour), the thinnest movement in the world at that time.
Piaget officially decides to produce watches exclusively in precious metals (gold or platinum).
Creation of the Legendary Gold, a bracelet with a finish that imitates the bark of a tree.
Creation of the famous Gold Coin watch, a secret coin watch with a case made from an American twenty-dollar gold piece.

1958: Birth of the "Piaget style," which requires the proportions of the case and bracelet to be in perfect harmony and shows great creativity in the decoration of the cases and dials.

Haute joaillerie Limelight jazz set. White gold, diamonds, and black spinel.
Secret watch with quartz movement Piaget 56P, 2010. © Piaget, photo Sébastian Coindre and Fabien Cruchon.

1959 : On June 15, the Piaget shop opens on 40, rue du Rhône, in Geneva.
Piaget expands its line to women's and men's jewellery and precious accessories.
Foundation of the Piaget Watch Corporation in New York to introduce the brand to the United States.

1960 : Piaget now signs its catalogues "watchmaker-jeweller" or "master watchmaker-jeweller," a testament to an operation that had now spread to *haute joaillerie* as a complement to the watch collections.
Self-winding Calibre 12P (19,800 vibrations/hour), the world's thinnest automatic movement at the time measuring a mere 2.35 mm thick, is introduced at the Basel Watch Fair.

1961 : Piaget starts to acquire several workshops which specialize in working with gold.

1963 : Creation of the 9154 reference model, which would later be called the "Protocole".

1964 : Piaget elevates semiprecious stones to the level of gemstones with the launch of its first watches with dials made from hard or semiprecious stones. Colour becomes the brand's signature: Coral, lapis lazuli, malachite, onyx, turquoise…up to thirty different stones. Piaget creations are recognizable at a glance, in complete harmony with the spirit of the 1960s.
Acquisition of Baume & Mercier, internationally renowned for its precision chronometers.

1967 : Piaget and the famous artist Salvador Dalí team up to develop the Dalí d'Or, a medal struck from 24-karat gold, issued in a limited series, and integrated into original jewellery. After studying watchmaking and gemology, Yves G. Piaget, Gérald's son, starts to work in the family firm's boutique in Geneva.

1968 : Yves G. Piaget is named director of marketing and communications.

1969 : Piaget participates in the creation of the first quartz movement fabricated in Switzerland, called Calibre Beta 21, at the *Centre électronique horloger* in Neuchâtel.
The *Comité du Bon Goût Français* awards Piaget its *Coupe d'Or*.
Creation of the first cuff watches for women.

1971 : The *Comité Français de l'Élite Européenne* awards Piaget the *Mercure de l'Élite Européenne*.

1972 : Piaget creates solitaire settings to highlight diamonds and shows off its expertise as a jeweller with its "Piaget diamond" certification.

1974 : Foundation of Prodor, which unites the various workshops Piaget had bought in Geneva.

1976 : The Polo World Cup, in West Palm Beach, is henceforth known as the Piaget World Cup.
The *Comité de l'Excellence Européenne* awards the brand the *Grand Prix Triomphe*.
Launch of the thinnest quartz movement at the time, the 7P.

1978 : Creation of the Geneva *Rose d'Or*, a gold rose awarded at the International New Rose Contest, in which Yves G. Piaget has participated since 1976.

1979 : Creation of the Piaget Polo watch, which significantly contributes to Piaget's success.

1982 : Production of the Phœbus, the most expensive men's watch bracelet of its time, with 296 diamonds, including a blue diamond, for a total of 87.87 carats, mounted on 154 grams of platinum to pay homage to the Greek god of the sun.

1984 : Creation of the Piaget d'Or by Swiss painter Hans Erni, struck by the Institut Fédéral des Monnaies. It is a coin that the House uses in pendants, bracelets, cuff links, and, of course, watches with an ultra-thin Calibre 4P.

1986 : Creation of the classic Dancer line.

1988 : Piaget joins with Cartier to later become a part of the Richemont Group.

1989 : Piaget sponsors the Deauville Gold Cup and increases its presence in equine sports by also sponsoring the Piaget Gold Cup at the Hong Kong Jockey Club.
Creation of the *haute joaillerie* watch Aura, studded with emerald-cut diamonds.

1990 : Launch of the Possession line, which establishes the concept of jewellery in motion. Launch of the Tanagra collection of watches and jewels, given the name of a Greek village famous for its ancient terra-cotta statuettes.

1991 : Creation of *Collections privées Piaget* (Piaget Private Collections) by buying back from individuals or from international auctions some of the most meaningful pieces that had made history, not only for the House, but also for modern watchmaking.

1992 : *Montres et Merveilles*, the first exhibition of the Piaget private collections, is presented in Milan at the sumptuous Palazzo Reale, before being shown in Geneva in 1994 at the *Musée de l'horlogerie et de l'émaillerie* (museum of watchmaking and enamelwork). Presentation of a mysterious clock with three faces showing the hours, minutes, and paths of the Sun and Moon.
Limited five-hundred-piece edition of the Georges Piaget watch.

1993 : Launch of the Gouverneur collection with classic models for men and women.

1994 : To celebrate its 120th anniversary, the brand creates a jewelled pocket watch with minute repetition and a retrograde chronograph, and a *grande sonnerie* wristwatch.

1996 : Launch of Glancy, a collection of watches and jewellery with a hexagonal structure inspired by the Japanese philosophy that attaches special importance to the number six, symbol of the creation of the world and nature.

1997 : The city of Venice commissions Piaget to carry out a complete restoration of the world-renowned Piazza San Marco Clock Tower, built in 1499 by the Rainieris, father and son.

1998 : Piaget brings a very contemporary interpretation of the heart to the Piaget d'Or collection and its pieces of *haute joaillerie* creations.
Launch of the Miss Protocole collection, with interchangeable bracelets.
Launch of the Altiplano ultra-thin watch collection, with the new ultra-thin Calibre 430P.

1999 : On its five hundredth anniversary on February 1st, the entirely restored mechanism of the Piazza San Marco Clock Tower in Venice is presented in a room of the Palace of the Doges. For the occasion, Piaget creates an exceptional skeletonized chronograph in the blue and gold of the city of Venice.
To celebrate its 125th anniversary, the *manufacture* launches the Emperador Eight Days, with a jump-hour Calibre 125P and an eight-day power reserve. This model inaugurates the Emperador collection.

2000 : Piaget creates the Limelight collection, celebrating the glamour of Hollywood with its large pieces and jewel-encrusted surfaces.
Launch of Calibre 551P, a self-winding movement with power reserve and small seconds indicators.
Piaget asserts itself as the jeweller of motion and creates the Dancer jewellery collection around the principle of a mobile, diamond-studded ingot.
Creation of an outstanding necklace: A nest of baguette-cut diamonds (35.5 carats) holding one exceptional diamond (8.8 carats).

2001 : Inauguration of the Manufacture de Haute Horlogerie Piaget near Geneva (Plan-les-Ouates). It brings together over forty professions in the fields of watchmaking and jewellery and completes production of the watches from the movements made in La Côte-aux-Fées.

2003 : Launch of the collection Magic Gardens of Piaget, inspired by the gardens that the brand adopts as its creative concept.
Launch of the House's first tourbillon movement, the 600P; the thinnest tourbillon movement in the world (3.5 mm thick).
Launch of Calibre 561P, a self-winding movement with retrograde seconds.

2004 : Development of the Garden of the Senses collection, around the themes of gardens and the five senses.

2005 : A systematic communications campaign created in partnership with French artists Pierre & Gilles: a series of four portraits, displayed in magical gardens.
Launch of the Possession watch, inspired by the famous jewellery line.
Launch of the gem-set skeleton version of Calibre 600P, first tourbillon to be gem-set, keeping its record thinness at 3.5 mm.
Launch of the Calibre 438P, ultra-thin movement, 2.15 mm thick.

2006 : Presentation of the Limelight Party collection, around the theme of celebration.
Launch of Calibre 608P, a tourbillon movement featuring a carriage placed on the minute hand; Calibre 850P, a dual time zone, self-winding movement; and Calibre 450P, an ultra-thin movement with small seconds, 2.15 mm thick.

2007 : Launch of Calibre 880P, a dual time-zone, flyback chronograph movement, only 5.6 mm thick; and Calibre 838P, ultra-thin movement with small seconds and a power reserve of approximately sixty-two hours, 2.5 mm thick.

2008 : Presentation of the Limelight Paris–New York collection, inspired by the architecture and haute couture of these two great cities.
Launch of Calibre 855P, perpetual calendar movement, and the skeleton version of the 838P.
On June 17, opening of the Piaget Time Gallery. Located just above the Piaget boutique (at 40 Rue du Rhône, in Geneva) and designed by French architect Gérard Barrau, this new exhibition space allows the House to highlight its heritage.
The newly formed Pilara Piaget team distinguishes itself at the Triple Crown in Buenos Aires, the most demanding tournament in international polo.

2009 : Presentation of the Limelight Paradise collection, with a tropical island theme.
Launch of the Emperador Coussin Grande Lune watch, with a new mechanical complication movement, Calibre 860P.
Launch of Calibre 835P, regulator movement.
The House celebrates thirty years of the Piaget Polo line and once again becomes an important player in the sport of kings in the United States—in particular at Palm Beach, where the brand became famous at the start of the 1980s with the launch of the Piaget Polo watch.

2010 : Presentation of the Limelight Jazz collection.
On the occasion of the fiftieth anniversary of Calibre 12P, Piaget shines with two world records: firstly for the thinnest self-winding movement (1200P and 1208P) and secondly for the thinnest self-winding watch (Piaget Altiplano 43 mm).

Piaget

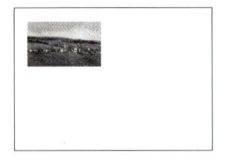

Engraving depicting La Côte-aux-Fées.
© Piaget Archives.

Family portrait. Georges Edouard Piaget, founder of Piaget, with his wife Emma and his fourteen children. © Piaget Archives.

Georges Edouard Piaget, founder of Piaget. © Piaget Archives.
Edouard, John, William, and Timothée Piaget. © Piaget Archives.

The Piaget Manufacture in La Côte-aux-Fées. In 1945, the first Piaget workshops made way for these vast premises designed for state-of-the-art watchmaking.
© Piaget Archives.
Piaget poster, 1948. © Piaget Archives.

Pocket watch in yellow gold. Mechanical movement, seventeen "lignes" engraved Piaget & Co.,1948. Piaget private collections. © Piaget Archives.
Gérald Piaget, grandson of the founder. © Piaget Archives.

The 9P movement, seen from the front and in profile, 2 mm thick, 1957.
© Piaget Archives.
Piaget poster, 1960. © Piaget Archives.

Assembly by a jeweller of the setting for a watch bracelet that will be part of a complete set. © Publi Conseil.
Jewellery watch in white gold set with brilliant-cut diamonds, marquise-cut diamonds, and cabochon rubies. Piaget 9P ultra-thin mechanical movement, 1978.
© Piaget Archives.

Self-winding 12P movement, 2.3 mm thick, 1960. © Piaget Archives.
Yellow gold watch. Piaget 12P, ultra-thin, self-winding mechanical movement, 1960. Piaget private collections. © Piaget, photo Fabien Cruchon.

Jewellery watch in white gold, wide bracelet with alternating onyx and turquoise, studded with diamonds. Piaget 9P ultra-thin mechanical movement, 1977. Piaget private collection. © Publi Conseil.
Dress by Capucci, Rome, 1970s. © Photo Peter Knapp.

Jewellery watch in white gold, bracelet set with diamonds and opals. Piaget 9P ultra-thin mechanical movement, 1972. Piaget private collections.
© Piaget, photo Fabien Cruchon.

Yves G. Piaget and Mireille Mathieu at the celebration of Piaget's one hundredth anniversary in Gstaad, 1974. © Piaget Archives.
Jewellery watch in yellow gold and red coral. Piaget 9P ultra-thin mechanical movement, 1974. Piaget private collections. © Piaget, photo Fabien Cruchon.

Yves G. Piaget, 1992. © Photo Frans Jansen.

Jackie Kennedy in Cambodia, 1967, in a dress by Valentino. © Max Scheler Estate, M. Scheler, Hamburg, Germany.
Piaget watch bought by Jackie Kennedy. Milanese bracelet in guilloche gold, diamond, and emerald-studded bezel, jade dial. Piaget 9P ultra-thin mechanical movement, 1965. Piaget private collections. © Piaget Archives.

Jewellery workshop. Setting the bracelet of a jewellery watch.
© Piaget Archives.

Jewellery set of white gold, onyx, and turquoise, set with diamonds, including necklace, earrings, ring, and a watch with a Piaget 4P mechanical movement, 1979.
© Piaget Archives.
Elizabeth Taylor, Rome, 1962. © Photo Bert Stern.

Gold coin watches with mechanisms housed inside an American twenty dollar coin, a Mexican twenty peso coin, and a Napoleon, 1957.
© Piaget Archives.

The artist Arman in his workshop, 1988.
© Piaget Archives.

Dalí What Makes You Tick? by Philippe Halsman, 1953.
© Philippe Halsman/Magnum Photos.
Secret watch made from a Dali d'Or. Piaget 9P ultra-thin mechanical movement, 1973. Piaget private collections. © Piaget, photo Fabien Cruchon.

Piaget advertisement from the 1970s. Yellow gold watch with coral dial set with diamonds. Piaget 9P ultra-thin mechanical movement.
© Piaget Archives.

Set of jewellery in yellow gold and tigereye comprised of a necklace, ring, and watch with a Piaget 9P ultra-thin mechanical movement, 1976. Piaget private collections.
© Piaget, photo Fabien Cruchon.

Piaget Polo watch with integrated bracelet and case. Launched in 1979, the Piaget Polo line contributed to the Piaget myth. Piaget 7P quartz movement. Piaget private collections. © Piaget, photo Sébastien Coindre.
Piaget World Cup, West Palm Beach, Florida, 1983.
© Piaget Archives.

Ursula Andress photographed with her Piaget Polo watch at the 1983 Piaget World Cup in Palm Beach. © Piaget Archives.
Piaget Polo watch. Piaget 7P quartz movement, 1979. Piaget private collections.
© Piaget, photo Sébastien Coindre.

Yves G. Piaget with the rose bearing his name. © Piaget Archives.
White gold ring with rose design, set with diamonds. © Piaget, photo Fabien Cruchon.

Platinum Phoebus watch, set with diamonds—including a 3.85 carat blue diamond of outstanding brilliance. Piaget 9P ultra-thin mechanical movement, 1982.
© Piaget Archives.

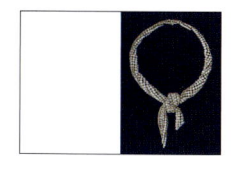

Haute joaillerie scarf necklace, 1984.
© Piaget Archives.

Limelight Paradise jewellery, including a white gold necklace set with diamonds, aquamarines, and tourmalines; and a white gold ring set with diamonds and an aquamarine, 2009.
© Piaget, photo Sébastien Coindre.

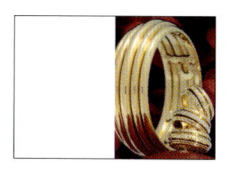

Possession jewellery: yellow gold rings set with diamonds, 1991; yellow gold bracelet, 1996. © Piaget Archives.

Piaget Altiplano watch in white gold. Piaget 430P ultra-thin mechanical movement, 2004. © Piaget, rights reserved.

Piaget Polo Tourbillon Relatif watch. Unique piece made of white gold, blue enamel, and mother-of-pearl, 608P mechanical movement, 2007.
© Piaget, photo Sébastien Coindre.
Clock tower, Piazza San Marco, Venice; **mechanism** for the clock from the Piazza San Marco, Venice; **clock detail**. © Piaget Archives.

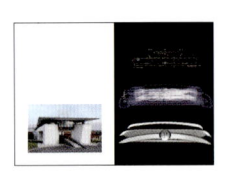

Manufacture de Haute Horlogerie Piaget, in Plan-les-Ouates. © Piaget Archives.
Integration of the 600P movement in the Piaget Emperador case. © Piaget Archives.

Piaget Limelight Magic Hour watch. Rotating bezel, three positions. Piaget 56P quartz movement, 2010. © Piaget, photo Olivier Currat.

Eiffel Tower seen at night. © Raimund Koch/Corbis.
Limelight Collection Paris–New York, 2008. © Piaget, photo Hervé Haddad.

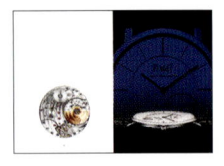

1208P movement. Thinnest self-winding, ultra-thin caliber in the world, 2.35 mm, 2009. © Piaget, photo Sébastien Coindre.
Piaget Altiplano watch in white gold, 5.25 mm thick. Launched in 2010, it beat the double record for the thinnest watch and automatic movement in the world.
© Piaget, photo Olivier Currat.

Piaget Polo Tourbillon Relatif watch. 608P manual winding mechanical movement, 2007. © Piaget, photo Sébastien Coindre.

Acknowledgments

The author would like to thank the House of Piaget for its help in the production of this work; in particular Yves G. Piaget and Philippe Léopold-Metzger, as well as the company personnel.

The publisher would like to thank the House of Piaget, as well as Frédéric Fritscher for his invaluable assistance. The publisher also wishes to thank Eva Bodinet (Magnum Photos), Cathy Cadenat (Corbis Images), Peter Knapp, Peer-Olaf Richter (Max Scheler Estate), and Bert Stern for their help in producing the pictures for this work.